ROUTLEDGE LI
PHONETICS A

Volume 14

FORMAL PHONOLOGY

FORMAL PHONOLOGY

ANDRÁS KORNAI

Routledge
Taylor & Francis Group

LONDON AND NEW YORK

First published in 1995 by Garland Publishing, Inc.

This edition first published in 2019
by Routledge
2 Park Square, Milton Park, Abingdon, Oxon OX14 4RN

and by Routledge
711 Third Avenue, New York, NY 10017

Routledge is an imprint of the Taylor & Francis Group, an informa business

British Library Cataloguing in Publication Data
A catalogue record for this book is available from the British Library

ISBN: 978-1-138-60364-6 (Set)
ISBN: 978-0-429-43708-3 (Set) (ebk)
ISBN: 978-1-138-32114-4 (Volume 14) (hbk)
ISBN: 978-1-138-32115-1 (Volume 14) (pbk)
ISBN: 978-0-429-45287-1 (Volume 14) (ebk)

Publisher's Note
The publisher has gone to great lengths to ensure the quality of this reprint but points out that some imperfections in the original copies may be apparent.

Disclaimer
The publisher has made every effort to trace copyright holders and would welcome correspondence from those they have been unable to trace.

FORMAL PHONOLOGY

ANDRÁS KORNAI

This is the PDF version of the book *Formal Phonology* published in the series
standing Dissertations in Linguistics, Garland Publishing, New York 1995, I
0-815-317301. Garland is now owned by Taylor and Francis, and an ISBN-1:
also been issued, 978-0815317302.

To my family

Contents

Preface

This work is primarily addressed to phonologists interested in speech and to speech engineers interested in phonology, two groups of people with very different expectations about what constitutes a convincing, rigorous presentation. The subject matter, the application of autosegmental theory for Markov modeling, is technical, but not really esoteric – autosegmental theory is at the core of contemporary phonology and Markov models are the main tool of speech recognition. Therefore it is hoped that anyone interested in at least one of these two fields will be able to follow the presentation, and perhaps find something useful here.

As the title indicates, this is a rather formal work. There are formal theorems stated throughout the text, and readers who do not have a good background in calculus and linear algebra will have to take these on faith. On the other hand, readers with a science or engineering background will find the proofs (which are generally relegated to the Appendices at the end of each chapter) reasonably simple, even enjoyable. The main body of the text is basically self-contained. It should be easy to follow for everyone familiar with the basics of set theory, logic, and automata theory. All three topics are amply covered for example in Barbara Partee, Alice ter Meulen, and Robert Wall's *Mathematical methods in linguistics* (Kluwer Academic, Dordrecht 1990). Except for the Appendices, formalism has been kept to an absolute minimum, with arguments and even theorems presented in an informal, discursive style. Concepts are frequently introduced without a rigorous definition. In such cases their first significant occurrence is given in *italics* and when they receive a formal definition they appear in **boldface**.

Phonologists are advised to read the main text sequentially, and perhaps to ignore all the Appendices except for 2.5.3. In section 0.2 of the Introduction a chapter by chapter summary of the results is provided to aid the readers in devising a reading plan better suited to their interests. No knowledge of Markov modeling is assumed, but readers completely unfamiliar with the subject might want to consult L.R. Rabiner and B.H. Juang's "Introduction to Hidden Markov Models" in the January 1986 issue of *IEEE ASSP Magazine,* pp. 4-16, or the more extensive collection of papers in chapter 6 of Alex Waibel and Kai-Fu Lee (eds) *Readings in speech recognition* (Morgan Kaufmann, San Mateo CA 1990).

Speech engineers are advised to go from the Introduction directly to the last chapter, and work their way backward to the extent they wish to learn about the formal theory of autosegmental phonology that provides the motivation for the structured Markov models presented in chapter 5. There is an Index of Definitions, and many backward pointers are provided in the text to make this reading plan feasible. No knowledge of autosegmental phonology is assumed, but the reader interested in the linguistic motivation and use of the ideas which are studied in the thesis in a rather abstract fashion might want to consult John Goldsmith's *Autosegmental and metrical phonology* (Basil Blackwell, Oxford 1990).

Most of the material presented here is taken from the author's 1991 Stanford dissertation with only stylistic changes. The most important exceptions are sections 1.4.5, 2.5.4, and 5.3.6, which are intended to bring the reader up to date by providing critical assessment of subsequent work. Some parts of the material have been published or submitted for publication elsewhere: in particular, section 4.4 is now available in a self-contained version as "The generative power of feature geometry" in the *Annals of Mathematics and Artificial Intelligence* **8** (1993) 37-46.

Introduction

0.1 The problem

The last twenty years have witnessed a profound split between the engineering and the theoretical aspects of the study of human speech. In speech engineering, and in particular in speech recognition, these years brought the ascendancy of unstructured, statistical models over the structured, rule-based models. In the same period phonological theory came to emphasize the abstract, structural properties of sound systems over the directly observable properties of sounds, and created a highly algebraic theory that almost entirely ignores the variability of actual speech. This split is nowhere more clear than in the use of distinctive features: in speech recognition virtually no model uses features, while in phonology practically all research takes place in a feature-based framework. Is there a way to make such a massively justified and widely used theoretical device as features useful for speech engineers? Could phonology benefit from such an undertaking? This is the subject matter of this book.

Speech engineers and computational linguists crave after efficiency; they do not believe there has been an advance in the state of the art until they have seen a better implementation, a faster algorithm. Yet it is often the case that no amount of engineering ingenuity can push a given approach beyond some local optimum – what is needed is an entirely new approach, a conceptual breakthrough. The field of speech recognition is precisely in this state: for the last ten or fifteen years each advance in Markov modeling yielded increasingly diminishing returns, and the goal of creating systems that perform large vocabulary, speaker independent, continuous speech recognition with the same efficiency as humans is nowhere in sight. Where can a conceptual breakthrough come from? The present work grew out of the conviction of the author that for speech engineering the best source of new conceptual machinery is phonology. The approach taken here is to formalize autosegmental phonology in order to create a theoretically sound conceptual framework for speech recognition with Markov models.

Markov models offer an extremely powerful learning mechanism which is especially well suited for data with inherent random variability, but one that is in no way specific to the nature of speech data. Triphone models cannot exploit the large scale language-specific regularities of the speech signal, such as vowel harmony or root-and-pattern paradigms, and they do not scale up to pentaphones and even larger domains where these regularities would become accessible. Furthermore, standard Markov models create a structural split between phonetics/phonology (captured in the individual triphones) and morphology (captured in the lexical network connecting the triphones) while linguistic theory tells us that phonology and morphology are part of the same (stratal) organization and operate in an interleaved fashion that permits no split. Present-day phonology/morphology, though conceptually better equipped to deal with these issues, unfortunately does not provide us with a large body of well-defined and highly optimized algorithms that can be readily put to use in a speech recognition system – in fact it hardly provides any algorithms at all. In its present state, phonology is not ready for optimization, but it is ready for *formalization*: the key ideas, developed in the phonological literature in an informal fashion[1], can be expressed in a more rigorous manner so that the results can serve as the conceptual basis for algorithmization.

---

[1] Pullum 1989 characterizes the informal style used in contemporary phonology as follows: "Even the best friends of the nonlinear phonology that has driven the relatively formal pre-1977-style segmental phonology into the wilderness (...) will admit that it isn't

0.2 The results

The most important overall result of this study is the creation of a model-theoretic framework that bridges the gap between the widely disparate practices of phonologists and speech engineers. Using this framework, the informally stated ideas of autosegmental phonology (AP) can be explicated, and the resulting model structures can serve as a blueprint in the design of speech recognition systems.

The syntactic devices used in expressing phonological generalizations are investigated in chapters 1 and 2, and the semantic interpretation of phonological representations is developed in chapters 3 and 4. The resulting model structures are then used as the basis of defining *structured Markov models* (sMMs) in chapter 5.

In the rest of this section the specific results are listed chapter by chapter and a brief discussion of their significance is provided. As can be seen from this list, the model-theoretic approach considerably improves the conceptual clarity of the often ill-understood technical devices used in phonological practice, and the design method stemming from it provides a completely new way of comparing and empirically testing a wide variety of specific proposals found in the phonological literature.

Main results of chapter 1

A.   The notion "well-formed autosegmental representation" is rigorously defined (1.1-1.3, 1.5). Significance: forms the basis of all that follows.

B.   A linear encoding of autosegmental representations (AR-s) is developed. Significance: standard two-level software, originally

---

trying to meet the conditions (...) for formal theories. True, a very significant outpouring of new ideas and new diagrammatic ways of attempting to express them has sprung up over the past decade; but it is quite clear that at the moment no one can say even in rough outline what a phonological representation comprises, using some exactly specified theoretical language. (...) Drifting this way and that in a sea of competing proposals for intuitively evaluated graphic representation does not constitute formal linguistic research, not even if interesting hunches about phonology are being tossed around in the process."

developed for the linear case, can now be used for AR-s.

C. Asymptotic formulas are established for the number of well-formed, as well as for fully associated AR-s, and an exact relationship between the two series of numbers is established (1.6). Significance: solves known open problem of enumerating AR-s, gives exact measure of the information content of AR-s, provides the basis for D below.

D. The non-existence of optimal linear encodings is demonstrated (1.4). Significance: Results in B are shown to be near-optimal, hopes for totally eliminating autosegmentalization squashed.

Main results of chapter 2

A. The notion "well-formed autosegmental rule" is rigorously defined (2.1-2.2). Significance: completes the syntactic reconstruction of AP, paves the way for generative capacity result E below.

B. Phonological theories of rule ordering reconstructed in uniform framework of finite state control (2.1). Significance: Protects result E below against objections based on rule ordering.

C. Classes of autosegmental automata defined (2.3, 2.5). Significance: theory of automata and formal languages can be extended to ARs.

D. Encoding of multi-tiered representations investigated, basic method of synchronization presented (2.4). Significance: forms the basis of the reconstruction of synchronization in chapter 4.

E. Kleene theorem for bistrings established, finite-state-ness of AP demonstrated (2.5). Significance: extends classical result of Johnson (1970) to autosegmental phonology, forms basis of F,G below.

F. Variety of extant theories of reduplication explained in light of generative capacity (2.5). Significance: explains the reasons for the failure of the existing theories.

G. Obligatory Contour Principle explained as the limiting (simplest) case of a range of possibilities available in finite-state systems (2.5). Significance: puts debate on OCP in new light.

Main results of chapter 3

A. Klatt's deterministic model of duration reinterpreted as a probabilistic model predicting upshifted lognormal duration density (3.1). Significance: provides theoretical justification for C below.

B. Haskins Labs' deterministic model of duration reinterpreted as a probabilistic model predicting lognormal duration density (3.2). Significance: provides theoretical justification for C below and links the phasepoint/lag theory of synchronization presented in 4.2 to well-established phonetic theory.

C. Instead of the widely used normal model, a lognormal model of duration is proposed (3.3). Statistical proof of superiority of lognormal over normal obtained (3.3). Significance: lognormal provides a new, theoretically justified way of explicitly controlling duration density in semi-markov models.

D. The duration densities of the most important topologies of tied-state Markov models are found to converge to Dirac-delta (3.4.1-3.4.2). Significance: increased frame rate is shown to be disadvantageous for models without input probabilities.

E. Models with initial probabilities are shown to be trainable to fit any prescribed duration density distribution (3.4.3). Significance: replaces the complex probabilities used by Cox with real numbers in the [0,1] range, provides theoretical justification for input models.

F. Model structures containing random variables are introduced (3.5). Significance: the use of random variables is the key technical innovation needed for describing the meaning of ARs in a model-theoretic framework.

Main results of chapter 4

A. A general theory of features, based in natural classes, is developed (4.1). Significance: provides unified treatment of SPE, Pāṇini, and feature geometry, paves the way for E below.

B. The phasepoint/lag formalism of synchronization is introduced (4.2). Significance: provides the semantics for association lines.

C. Interval systems and interval structures defined (4.3). Significance: completes model-theoretic reconstruction of AP, forms the basis of sMMs presented in chapter 5.

D. Role of non-convexity and non-monotonicity in phonological theory investigated (4.3). Significance: underlying causes of nonmonotonicity exposed.

E. Weakly boolean structures (Ehrenfeucht) are used to justify feature geometry (4.4). Significance: puts feature geometry in new light, makes relationship between contemporary and earlier theories clear.

Main results of chapter 5

A. Segmental interpretation is presented (5.1). Significance: provides the theoretical underpinnings for standard Markov models.

B. Cascade construction of sMMs introduced (5.2). Significance: captures the lack of synchrony among the features.

C. The possibility of training feature detectors is demonstrated (5.2). Significance: model need not rely on human expertise.

D. Recursive construction of sMMs according to a given feature geometry explained (5.3). Significance: enables linguist to choose between competing geometries on the basis of speech recognition performance.

E. Evaluation criteria for sMMs are presented (5.4). Significance: sMMs are a new class of Markov models, expected to be very successful in speech recognition. They are theoretically justified by AP, but unproven in practice.

0.3 The method

This work belongs in a broad scientific tradition, starting perhaps with Euclid, and probably best exemplified in modern linguistics by the early work of Chomsky, of using formal tools as a means of extending our knowledge about an empirical domain. In the first four chapters, the key ideas of autosegmental phonology are explicated[2], and in chapter 5 the resulting formal system is used for the construction of structured Markov models in order to link the actual practice of phonologists to the actual practice of speech engineers. No ink will be wasted on criticizing the lack of mathematical rigor in phonology, or the lack of theoretical orientation in speech engineering, as the author believes that more can be gained from trying to integrate the positive contributions of both fields than from trying to get people do things 'properly'.

---

[2]The task of *explication* consists in transforming a given more or less inexact concept into an exact one or, rather, replacing the first by the second. We call the given concept (or the term used for it) the *explicandum*, and the exact concept proposed to take the place of the first (or the term proposed for it) the *explicatum*. The explicandum may belong to everyday language or to a previous stage in the development of scientific language. The explicatum must be given by explicit rules for its use, for example, by a definition which incorporates it into a well-constructed system of scientific either logicomathematical or empirical concepts. (...)

A problem of explication is characteristically different from ordinary scientific (logical or empirical) problems, where both the datum and the solution are, under favorable conditions, formulated in exact terms (for example, 'What is the product of 3 and 5?', 'What happens when an electric current goes through water?'). In a problem of explication the datum, viz., the explicandum, is not given in exact terms; if it were, no explication would be necessary. Since the datum is inexact, the problem itself is not stated in exact terms; and yet we are asked to give an exact solution. This is one of the puzzling peculiarities of explication. It follows that, if a solution for a problem of explication is proposed, we cannot decide in an exact way whether it is right or wrong. Strictly speaking, the question whether the solution is right or wrong makes no good sense because there is no clear-cut answer. The question should rather be whether the proposed solution is satisfactory, whether it is more satisfactory than another one, and the like. (Carnap 1950)

This emphasis on the positive contributions sets the present work apart from earlier attempts at developing a formal system of phonology and morphology. Categorial phonology (Wheeler 1981) and morphology (Hoeksema 1985), finite-state phonology and morphology (Kaplan and Kay ms, Koskenniemi 1983), or the more recent work on autosegmental phonology at Edinburgh (Bird and Klein 1990, Scobbie 1991) are certainly rigorous enough to satisfy even the most demanding taste. However, these systems do not offer a formal *reconstruction* of mainstream generative phonology, they offer formal *alternatives*. Because they explicitly reject one or more of the fundamental assumptions underlying the sequential mode of rule application used in the vast majority of generative phonological analyses, they do not make it possible to restate the linguists' work in a formal setting – in order to enjoy the benefits of the formal rigor offered by these systems one must reanalyze the data.

The orientation of the present work is exactly the opposite: rather than championing the merits of any particular assumption, the aim is to create a meta-level formalism which is abstract enough to carry the often contradictory versions of AP as special cases. The definitions of well-formedness (section 1.3), rule ordering (section 2.1), rule types (section 2.2), HMM topologies (section 3.2), and feature geometries (section 4.1) are all made in this spirit. There are, to be sure, cases where the author cannot hide his sympathies completely, but the aim is to keep these to a minimum so that most autosegmental analyses can be faithfully replicated. It follows from this strategy that devices unique to a particular version of AP will not be analyzed in great detail; tools of the theory such as a reduplicative CVC template are not taken to be primitives but are built from the primitives supplied by the abstract framework. The advantage of this abstract outlook is that the work is not tied to any particular, and thus soon to be outdated, version of phonological theory.

Since the the reader will not encounter sMMs until the last chapter, in a sense the bulk of this formal work is preparatory in nature. Given the rather wide-spread sentiment in speech engineering that linguistic models do not work and that it is altogether better to replace human intuitions about speech by automatically extracted knowledge (see e.g. Makhoul and Schwartz 1986), the question will no doubt be asked: why bother with all this theory? From the perspective of the speech engineer, the complexity of our preparations, and indeed the complexity of present-day phonological theory, can only be justified if it gives rise to more success-ful applications. But from the perspective of the phonologist the first four chapters are not preparatory at all; formalizing phonological theory is a worthwhile undertaking that can advance our conceptual understand-ing of language quite independently of its utility for speech recognition, speech synthesis, voice compression, speaker identification, or any other practical task confronting the speech engineer. The rest of this section discusses the logical structure of this undertaking, which is largely inde-pendent of the organization imposed by the specific results summarized in section 0.2 above. Readers more interested in the results than in broad metatheoretical considerations can skip this discussion without great loss.

What does phonological theory do? *How* does it do it? *Why* does it do it that particular way? These are the questions a detailed formalization should seek to answer. As for the first of these questions, most practicing phonologists view their theory as an instrument that will, much like the physician's X-ray machine, make accessible a well-defined part of the internal structure in humans that enables them to pursue a certain kind of activity, namely communication by means of conventional sounds or handsigns. And as an ordinary X-ray machine will bring into sharp relief the bones, and tell us little about the muscles, nerves, and other soft tissue equally important for the task of locomotion, phonological theory is focussed on a single component of communication, namely the *mental representations* associated with the sound/handsign aspect of the message communicated. Thus the first chapter is devoted to an explication of the mental representations assumed in contemporary phonological theory.

The second question, how phonology makes mental representations of the sound (or handsign) aspect of language accessible, is perhaps best understood from the perspective of writing and transcription systems. The move from mora-based or syllable-based to alphabetic writing systems introduces an abstract kind of unit that cannot be pronounced in isolation, namely (oral) stop consonants. The move from alphabetic to feature-based transcription (intimately linked with the early history of phonetics/phonology, see e.g. Jespersen's 1889 critique history of phonetics/phonology, see e.g. Jespersen's 1889 critique of Sweet 1880) results in completely abstract, unpronounceable units which embody the mental unity of articulatory and acoustic specifications (Jakobson, Fant and Halle 1952, Halle 1983). These units, and larger structures composed from them, can be made accessible via the study of the grammatical rules and constraints that are stated in their terms. Thus the second chapter is devoted to an explication of the rule and constraint systems used in contemporary phonological theory.

The third question, why phonology concentrates on the grammatical manifestation of mental units at the expense of their physical manifestations, has only a partial answer: the physical phenomena associated with speech are extremely complex, and their experimental investigation poses serious problems. As long as phonological derivations cannot be directly verified (because the nerve impulse patterns corresponding to the activation of mental units in the production and perception of spoken or signed language cannot be followed through the central nervous system), phonologists will have to rely on indirect evidence of some sort. But the difficulties in obtaining experimental evidence can only partially explain why contemporary phonology relies almost exclusively on grammatical evidence and why, in the rare cases when physical evidence is admitted, the articulatory domain is so strongly preferred.

The first major exposition of standard generative phonology, Chomsky and Halle 1968, devotes a full chapter to listing "the individual features that together represent the phonetic capabilities of man" but grounds the features only on articulatory correlates, mentioning "the acoustical and perceptual correlates of a feature only occasionally, not because we regard these aspects as either less interesting or less important, but rather because such discussions would make this section, which is itself a digression from the main theme of our book, much too long" (p 299). The most influential textbook of standard generative phonology, Kenstowicz and Kisseberth 1979, defines acoustic phonetics (p 7) but discusses only articulatory theory under the heading "linguistic phonetics" (pp 7-23). Expositions of the modern generative theory of features, such as Sagey 1986, again discuss articulatory, but not acoustic, evidence. Chapters 3 and 4 of this book are based on the view that the historical reasons for giving preference to grammatical over articulatory over acoustic data are no longer valid.

While it was certainly true a hundred years or even a few decades ago that careful observation of speech production yielded more reliable data than the "trained ear", and that elicitation or introspection yielded even more reliable, quantized data about grammaticality judgments, neither of these points remains valid today. The recording and precise tracking of the position of the articulators during speech production is a major undertaking requiring specialized equipment of the sort described in Fujimura, Kiritani and Ishida 1973, while the recording and analysis of digitized speech can be performed on equipment no more complex than a personal computer. Furthermore, the inherently continuous and variable nature of speech data is brought under control by quantization and other modern statistical techniques, while the inherently quantized and invariable nature of grammaticality judgments becomes less and less pronounced as attention is shifted from the ideal speaker-hearer of the ideally homogeneous speech community to actual speakers in actual communities. Therefore, rather than excluding acoustic evidence from the domain of phonology, we should endeavor to create a "phonetic interpretation" that will map discrete phonological representations to physical events that unfold in real time.

The existing theories of phonetic interpretation, such as Keating 1988, Bird and Klein 1990, have two main shortcomings. First, they link phonological features to articulatory specifications and thus presume a thorough understanding of the relationship between the positions of the articulators and the acoustic signal. Second, they only describe the timing of (the beginning and end of) each gesture relative to (the beginning and end of) other gestures, but give no information about the absolute value of the time lags or the duration of the gestures. The theory developed in this book overcomes both of these shortcomings: it is applicable to all kinds of dynamically changing parameter vectors (be they articulatory, e.g. derived from X-ray microbeam records, or acoustic, e.g. derived by the kinds of digital signal processing techniques discussed in Rabiner and Schaefer 1979) and it is real time.

As a result of the work undertaken in the first four chapters, autosegmental phonology, and its phonetic interpretation, become a formal, readily algorithmizable theory of speech. However, it still suffers from a problem not much appreciated by linguists but taken very seriously by speech engineers: it is totally dependent on human expertise. In addition to the underlying representations and the rules, the grammarian will also have to specify the parameters of the interpretation. Since the number of such parameters is quite large, an automatic method of extracting them is clearly desirable. Chapter 5 is devoted to a new class of hidden Markov models which make it possible to perform parameter extraction (training) of phonologically motivated models using existing technology.

0.4   References

Bird, Steven and Ewan H. Klein 1990. Phonological events. *Journal of Linguistics* **26** 33–56.

Carnap, Rudolf 1950. *Logical foundations of probability*. University of Chicago Press.

Chomsky, Noam and Morris Halle 1968. *The Sound Pattern of English*. Harper & Row, New York.

Fujimura, Osamu, S. Kiritani and H. Ishida 1973.   Computer controlled radiography for observation of movements of articulatory and other human organs. *Computer Biological Medicine* **3** 371–384.

Halle, Morris 1983.   Distinctive features and their articulatory implementation. *Natural Language and Linguistic Theory* **1** 91–107.

Hoeksema, Jack 1985.   *Categorial Morphology*. Garland Publishing, New York.

Jakobson, Roman, Gunnar Fant and Morris Halle 1952.   *Preliminaries to speech analysis: the distinctive features and their correlates.* MIT Press, Cambridge MA.

Jespersen, Otto   1889.   The articulations of speech sounds, Marburg.

Kaplan, Ronald and Martin Kay ms.   *Phonological rules and finite state transducers.* Xerox PARC.

Keating, Patricia A. 1988.   Underspecification in phonetics. *Phonology* **5** 275–292.

Kenstowicz, Michael and Charles Kisseberth 1979.   *Generative Phonology*. Academic Press, New York.

Koskenniemi, Kimmo   1983.   Two-level Morphology: a general computational model for word-form recognition and production, Department of General Linguistics, University of Helsinki Publication, Helsinki.

Makhoul, John and Richard Schwartz 1986.   Ignorance modeling. In *Invariance and Variability of Speech Processes*, Joseph S. Perkell and Dennis H. Klatt, (eds.) Lawrence Erlebaum Associates, Hillsdale, NJ, 344–345.

Pullum, Geoffrey K. 1989.   Formal linguistics meets the Boojum. *Natural Language and Linguistic Theory* **7** 137–143.

Rabiner, L. and R. Schaefer 1979.   *Digital processing of speech signals.* Prentice Hall, Englewood Cliffs NJ.

Sagey, Elizabeth 1986. *The representation of features and relations in non-linear phonology.* PhD Thesis, MIT.

Scobbie, James M. 1991. *Attribute Value Phonology.* PhD Thesis, University of Edinburgh.

Sweet, Henry 1880. Sound notation. *Transactions of the Philological Society* **2**.

Wheeler, Deirdre W. 1981. *Aspects of a categorial theory of phonology.* PhD Thesis, UMASS Amherst.

Acknowledgments

It is a pleasure to acknowledge my indebtedness to
Tryg Ager `<tryg@csli.stanford.edu>`,
Jared Bernstein `<jared@wrl.epi.com>`,
David Boyes `<dboyes@brazos.rice.edu>`,
Becky Burwell `<burwell@parc.xerox.com>`,
Marcia Bush `<bush@parc.xerox.com>`,
Corky Cartwright `<cork@cs.rice.edu>`,
Cleo Condoravdi `<conclea@yalevm.bitnet>`,
Vicky Dean `<rif@cs.rice.edu>`,
Andrzej Ehrenfeucht `<andrzej@piper.cs.colorado.edu>`,
Tim Fernando `<fernando@csli.stanford.edu>`,
Jeff Goldberg `<goldberg@nytud.hu>`,
Louis Goldstein `<goldstein@yalehask.bitnet>`,
József Hollósi `<hollosi@hix.com>`,
Arthur House `<house%idacrd@princeton.edu>`,
Sharon Inkelas `<inkelas@garnet.berkeley.edu>`,
Don Johnson `<dhj@rice.edu>`,
Doug Jones `<jones@cogito.mit.edu>`,
Dikran Karagueuzian `<dikran@csli.stanford.edu>`,
Lauri Karttunen `<lauri.karttunen@xerox.fr>`,
Paul Kiparsky `<kiparsky@csli.stanford.edu>`,
János Kornai `<kornai@zeus.colbud.hu>`,
Péter Lakner `<plakner@gsb.nyu.edu>`,

Teréz Laky <h8484lak@ella.hu>,
Will Leben <leben@russell.stanford.edu>,
Alan Manne <asm@sierra.stanford.edu>,
Katy McKinin <katya@ricevm1.rice.edu>,
Michelle Murray <michelle@csli.stanford.edu>,
Bich Nguyen <btn@itstd.sri.com>,
Joseph Olive <jpo@research.att.com>,
John Paolillo <johnp@utaf11.uta.edu>,
Emma Pease <emma@csli.stanford.edu>,
Stanley Peters <peters@csli.stanford.edu>,
Chris Pinon <pinon@csli.stanford.edu>,
Livia Polányi <polanyi@ricevm1.rice.edu>,
Bill Poser <poser@crystals.stanford.edu>,
Geoff Pullum <gkp@ucscc.ucsc.edu>,
Alan Prince <prince@ruccs.rutgers.edu>,
Jan van Santen <jphvs@research.att.com>,
Josef Schreiner <csilla@netcom.com>,
Jim Scobbie <scobbie@csli.stanford.edu>,
Donca Steriade <ibenajt@mvs.oac.ucla.edu>,
Kari Swingle <swingle@ling.ucsc.edu>,
Steven Tepper <greep@speech.sri.com>,
Rich Thomason <thomason@cad.cs.cmu.edu>,
Sally Thomason <sgt@a.nl.cs.cmu.edu>,
Bob Wall <lifz050@utxvms.cc.utexas.edu>,
Gina Wein <wein@csli.stanford.edu>,
Iván Weisz <weisz@math.ohio-state.edu>,
Michael Wescoat <wescoat@csli.stanford.edu>,
Deirdre Wheeler <dww@speech1.cs.cmu.edu>,
Meg Withgott <withgott@interval.com>,
Annie Zaenen <zaenen@parc.xerox.com>,
Draga Zec <dzec@yalevm.bitnet>,
Arnold Zwicky <zwicky@csli.stanford.edu>,

and collectively to `ling-faculty`, `ling-grads`, `ling-staff`, and `pinterest@csli.stanford.edu`.

It would be foolish to attempt ranking these people according to their degree of supportiveness or the nature of their contributions. But let me single out those to whom I owe the most: my wife Livia, my son Michael, and my parents János and Teréz. This work is dedicated to them.

Formal Phonology

Chapter 1

Autosegmental representations

The aim of this chapter is to describe in a rigorous manner the basic data structures of phonological theory, called *autosegmental representations.* Section 1.1 discusses the atomic elements of the representations, *distinctive features,* and sections 1.2 and 1.3 introduce the *tiers* and *association lines* that are used to collect the atoms into more complex representations. These sections provide a series of definitions to replace the phonologist's intuitive judgment of whether a tentative autosegmental representation is well-formed or not by an algorithmic procedure that can be used to check well-formedness mechanically.

In addition to providing the conceptual basis for implementation, the formal treatment opens the way to investigating autosegmental representations in an abstract manner. The first results of such an investigation are presented in section 1.4, where it is shown that autosegmental representations can be represented as linear strings in a near-optimal manner. This linear encoding will play a crucial role both in the discussion of *hierarchical structure* in section 1.5 and in the description of *rules,* which is the subject matter of chapter 2.

The formal definitions presented in the first two chapters can be thought of as a proposal concerning the rules and representations permitted by Universal Grammar. The emphasis is on presenting current phonological practice in a formal setting, and little effort has been made to incorporate substantive universals. The inventory of rules and representations developed here is sufficiently rich to serve as a basis for the discussion of the complex (and sometimes contradictory) models employed in contemporary phonology/morphology, but in spite of this richness, it will provide a surprisingly strict upper bound on the complexity of Universal Phonology.

1.1   Subsegmental structure

A key point, common to SPE (Chomsky and Halle 1968) and autosegmental phonology (Goldsmith 1990), is that segments can be further decomposed into atomic units called *distinctive features* or just *features*.[1] These features can be thought of as classificatory devices that group the phonemes into classes. Under this *instrumentalist* view features are abstract properties of phonemes much the same way as [square-free] or [odd] are abstract properties of integers, and their *raison d'être* is to be found in the usefulness of the classification they induce rather than in direct articulatory and/or acoustic correlates, be these absolute (as for [voiced]) or relative (as for [strident]). From this perspective, a feature will refer to some global property of segments and it makes little or no sense to attribute temporal extent to it.

Nevertheless, it is often possible and indeed desirable to think of features such as [labial] as constituent parts of segments. Under this *realist* view, features are concrete parts of the phonemes in much the same way as prime factors are the constituent parts of natural numbers. In the articulatory domain, the realist view implies that the gesture corresponding to

---

[1]For our purposes, the distinctiveness of the atomic units is of secondary importance. Therefore, I will simply use the term *feature* and talk of *distinctive* features only where the idea of distinctiveness is especially relevant.

a phoneme is basically the sum of the articulatory gestures corresponding to its constituent features (Halle 1983), and in the acoustic domain it implies that there exist cues corresponding to any feature such as [labial] that will be invariant across phonemes such as *b* or *m* that share the feature in question (Stevens and Blumstein 1981). From this perspective, the temporal organization of features within and across segments becomes a relevant issue, and linear (SPE) and non-linear (autosegmental) phonology differ primarily in the way features are located in time. In the linear theory, all features are coterminous with the segment they characterize, while in the non-linear theory they can be restricted to various stretches of the segments. The synchronization mechanisms that create and maintain these restrictions are the subject of chapter 4 – here it will be sufficient to give a simple but typical example.

In tone languages such as Mende (Leben 1978), where short vowels can carry contour tones, linear phonology assumed dynamic tone features such as [falling tone]. Autosegmental phonology uses only static features such as [high tone] and [low tone], (standardly abbreviated H and L) and represents the falling tone by

(1)

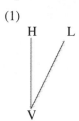

Here V stands for the vowel bearing the falling tone, and H and L are features on a tonal *tier* which are *associated* to the vowel which is located on a different tier. Informally speaking, the vowel has the property H followed by the property L, i.e. it starts out as bearing high tone but (gradually) turns into bearing low tone. As a first step towards making this idea more rigorous, the notions of tier and association will be defined next in sections 1.2 and 1.3, respectively.

1.2   Tiers

In autosegmental phonology, representations are displayed as three-dimensional structures which have a characteristic left-to-right axis corresponding, conceptually, to the flow of time. Roughly speaking, features on a line parallel to this axis constitute a *tier*, while features on a plane perpendicular to the axis are arranged in a tree structure called the *geometry* of the features. Here we will select a single 'plane' defined by two adjacent tiers, and defer the discussion of 'geometry' until section 1.5.

If the features and association lines of autosegmental phonology are conceptualized as (labeled) vertices and (undirected, unlabeled) edges, two-tiered representations will correspond to partially labeled bipartite graphs where each partition (tier) is endowed with a linear ordering $<$ and the edges satisfy the so-called *No Crossing Constraint* (Goldsmith 1976) or NCC for short: if (x, y) and (x', y') are edges, and $x < x'$ holds, then $y < y'$ must also hold.

Such graphs can be trivially embedded in the (euclidean) plane by positioning the vertices in one partition (tier) on lattice points of the line $y = 0$, and the vertices in the other tier on lattice points on the line $y = 1$. The orderings correspond to the natural left-to-right ordering of these lines, and the edges can be depicted as straight line segments between the vertices. These line segments will never cross at an internal point – hence the name No Crossing Constraint.

In order to describe the concept of a *tier* more fully, we have to provide some further detail about the node labels. Informally, a tier is a place where we can store strings of node labels (over some finite alphabet called the **tier alphabet** T) or sequences of such strings (called the **melodies** belonging to the words of a given phrase) in such a manner that adjacent elements within one melody can be accessed one after the other and adjacent melodies can also be accessed one after the other. There are no *a priori* limits on the length or the number of melodies, so we will use the oldest (and simplest) abstract model of infinite storage, *Turing machine tapes,* as our mathematical model of tiers.

Turing machine **tapes** are composed of elementary *cells* each of which initially contains a distinguished **blank** symbol that we will denote by G. This symbol can be replaced by some other symbol, which in turn can be replaced by G or yet another symbol and so on. At any given time, a **cell** holds exactly one of a finite set of symbols and, unless some writing procedure is performed, will hold this symbol forever. To make a tape, the cells are doubly linked in a two-way infinite list – for convenience, we will index the cells by integers.

Definition 1. A **tier** is an ordered pair (Z,H) where Z is the set of integers equipped with the standard identity and ordering relations '$=$' and '$<$' and H is the *name* of the tier.

The definition puts no restriction on the syntax of tier names, but I will usually use the letters H,I,J,... rather than contentful expressions like *segmental, tonal, backness, timing, voicing* etc. Clearly, two tiers bearing identical names can only be distinguished by inspecting their contents. Let us define a tier **containing** a string $t_0 t_1 ... t_n$ starting at position k by a mapping that maps k on t_0, $k+1$ on t_1 ,..., $k+n$ on t_n and everything else on G. Abstracting away from the starting position, we get

Definition 2. A tier H containing a melody $t_0 t_1 ... t_n$ over the alphabet T_H is defined as the class of mappings T_k that take $k+i$ into t_i for $0 \leq i \leq n$ and to G if i is outside this range. Unless noted otherwise, this class will be denoted by the uppercase version of the name of the string and will be represented by the mapping T_0.

In order to create a single string out of the melodies occupying different portions of the same tier, it will be expedient to adjoin the symbol G to every tier alphabet – the enlarged tier alphabet will be denoted by T_G. By defining the relation of **(technical) equivalence** on strings over T_G as the minimal equivalence in which G and GG are equivalent, we can capture the idea that the melodies of adjacent morphemes are adjacent while retaining the distinction between tautomorphemic and heteromorphemic tones.[2] Given two melodies such as HL and HLH, HLGHLH will be technically equivalent to HLGGHLH, HLGGGHLH, and so on, meaning these are heteromorphemic melodies. However, it will not be equivalent to the tautomorphemic HLHLH, because G is not the empty string but an actual symbol in the (enlarged) alphabet.

In terms of Turing machine tapes, these definitions mean that we can think of a tier containing some melodies m_i in the same way that we think about a tape on which the strings m_i are separated from one another by some blanks. Technical equivalence was introduced above to assure that the number of blanks between adjacent melodies is immaterial[3]. In phonological practice strings are often separated by explicit boundary markers, and in some cases the number of such boundary symbols, for example, # vs. ##, is important. For our purposes, such boundary symbols are contentful elements to be added to the tier alphabet independent of G – we will return to this matter in 1.5 below.

1.3　Association

Let us start with a tier H containing the melody h = $h_0 h_1 ... h_n$ and a tier S containing the melody s = $s_0 s_1 ... s_m$. It does not matter whether the two tier alphabets are disjoint – we might suppose without loss of generality that the only symbol in their intersection is G. An **association line** is defined simply as a pair (i, j), this will be depicted by a line connecting s_i in the string s to h_j in the string h. As mentioned earlier, these pairs are unordered – in other words, we do not allow directed association lines. Moreover, neither s_i nor h_j can be G – in other words, we do not allow 'dangling' association lines[4]. An **association relation** will be

---

[2]The approach taken here should be contrasted to that of Bird and Klein 1989, which uses explicit boundary markers ('point events') to encode the beginning and end of items (see Kornai 1989 and 2.5.4 below).

[3]Using phonological terminology we might say that equivalence ensures that the blank squares of the tape satisfy the OCP, which will be discussed in 2.5.3.

[4]This restriction limits the expressive power of the formalism; here the idea that two nodes share the value of a feature cannot be expressed without explicit reference to the value

defined as any set of association lines; as the melodies are finite, the relations will also have to be finite. A **bistring** is defined as an ordered triple (f, g, A), where f and g are strings not containing G, and A is an association relation over f and g. As we shall see in chapter 2, bistrings play the same role in formal autosegmental theory as strings in formal language theory.

An association relation A is **well-formed** iff it contains no pairs (i, k) (j, l) such that $i < j$ but $k > l$, i.e. iff it satisfies the No Crossing Constraint.

(2A)   (2B)

Excluding the crossing association pattern depicted in (2A) has the beneficial effect that the intended temporal interpretation, which takes association lines to mean temporal overlap (see Sagey 1988), can be coherently stated (see Bird and Klein 1990). By excluding further association patterns such as the configuration depicted in (3), the representations can be brought into even closer alignment with phonological intuition.

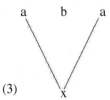

(3)

Intuitively, configurations like (3) can correspond to a single discontinuous a that is interrupted by the b or to a sequence of three uninterrupted (convex) events a, b, and a. It is not always clear which interpretation is

---

of the feature that is being shared. The attribute-value formalism developed in Scobbie 1991 is capable of expressing the idea of higher nodes sharing a value for a lower one – whether this additional expressive power is needed in phonology remains to be seen.

the appropriate one, and at certain stages of the derivation, especially near the end, we might wish to exclude such configurations. A well-formed representation not containing this configuration will be called **proper**. Let us define the **span** of an element x as with respect to some association relation A as those elements y for which (x,y) is in A. In proper representations, the span of an element will always be a single substring of the melody on the other tier (a weaker but phonologically more relevant notion of proper-ness will be introduced via *projections* shortly).

Finally, those bistrings in which every element is in the domain or range of the association relation will be called **fully associated**. Fully associated well-formed bistrings are obviously proper, but the converse is not true: the bistring in (4) is well-formed and proper but not fully associated.

(4)

Elements that are unassociated, such as b in (3) or a in (4) are often called *floating*. In the final stage of the derivation, SPE phonology required fully specified feature structures. Similarly, most varieties of autosegmental phonology require fully associated representations at least in the last step of the derivation, and often earlier. But floating elements and not proper representations will often be indispensable in earlier stages of the derivation, and even ill-formed representations are legitimate data structures in those versions of autosegmental theory where the NCC is viewed only as a tendency as in Bagemihl 1989.

Our definition of bistrings (and in general k-strings, see 1.5 below) is largely comparable to the graph-theoretically inspired definition given in Coleman and Local 1991, which takes k-tiered autosegmental representations to be k-partite graphs with nodes corresponding to features and edges corresponding to association lines. But there is an important difference in that our definition treats melodies as given, so that the structures in (2A) and (2B) above are not equivalent: (2A) is ill-formed and (2B) is well-formed. Another problem with abandoning the melodies as fundamental elements of autosegmental representations is that in purely graph-theoretic terms temporal sequencing would make no sense. But in the language-theoretic formalization presented here temporal sequencing and reversal are natural developments.

Definition 3. Given two bistrings (f, h, A) and (k, l, B) on tiers N and M, their **concatenation** (fk, hl, AB) is constructed via their respective tier-alphabet functions $F_0, H_0, K_{|f|}$, and $L_{|h|}$ as follows. $FK_0(i) = F(i)$ for $0 \leq i < |f|$, $K_{|f|}(i)$ for $|f| \leq i < |f| + |k|$, G otherwise. $HL_0(j) = H(j)$ for $0 \leq j < |k|$, $L_{|h|}(j)$ for $|k| \leq j < |h| + |l|$, G otherwise. Finally, the concatenation of A and B, denoted AB, is defined as $A \cup \{(i + |f|, j + |k|) \mid (i, j) \in B\}$

Notice that the concatenation of two connected bistrings will not be connected (as a bipartite graph). This is remedied by the following

Definition 4. Given two bistrings as above, their **t-catenation** (resp. **b-catenation**) is defined as (fk, hl, AtB) (resp. (fk, hl, AbB)), where $AtB = AB \cup \{(|f| - 1, |k|)\}$ and $AbB = AB \cup \{(|f|, |k| - 1)\}$. Using phonological terminology, in t-catenation the last element of the top tier of the first bistring is spread on the first element of the bottom tier of the second bistring, and in b-catenation the last element of the bottom tier of the first string is spread on the first element of the top tier of the second bistring.

The only autosegmental operation that is not the straightforward generalization of some well-known string operation is that of **alignment**. Given two bistrings $x = (f, g, A)$ and $y = (g, h, B)$, their alignment $z = x \sim y$ is defined to be (f, h, C), where C is the relation-composition of A and B; in other words, the pair (i, k) will be in C iff there is some j such that (i, j) is in A and (j, k) is in B. Now we are in a position to define projections: these involve some subset S of the tier alphabet T.

A **projector** $P_S(h)$ of a string $g = h_0 h_1 ... h_m$ with respect to a set S is the bistring (h, h, SXS), where (i, j) is in SXS iff $i = j$ and h_i is in S. The **normal bistring** $I(h)$ corresponding to a string h is simply its projector with respect to the full alphabet: $I(h) = P_T(h)$. A **projection** of a string with respect to some subalphabet S can now be defined as the alignment of the corresponding normal bistring with the projector.

The alignment of well-formed bistrings-strings is not necessarily well-formed, as the following example shows. Let $f = ab, g = c, h = de$ and suppose that the following associations hold: $(0, 0)$ and $(1, 0)$ in x, $(0, 0)$ and $(0, 1)$ in y. By definition, C should contain $(0, 0), (0, 1), (1, 0)$, and $(1, 1)$ and will thus violate the NCC. (For a discussion of the possible approaches to this and similar cases of well-formedness violations see 2.2.) I will say that a bistring (f, h, A) is **proper with respect to a subset** S **of the tier-alphabet** T (underlying the string h), iff $(f, h, A) \sim P_S(h)$ is proper. As we shall see in chapter 4.3, it is this relativized notion of proper-ness (relativized with respect to the set of 'P-bearing units', see Clements and Ford 1979) that plays a role in phonology.

1.4 Linearization

Using the primitive operations of concatenation, **association** i.e. (adding a pair to the association relation), and **delinking** (i.e. subtracting a pair from the association relation), a large and important part of autosegmental phonology, including all the early work on tone and harmony, can be faithfully reconstructed in the framework developed so far.[5] But before we can turn to this task in chapter 2, we will need one more formal tool, namely a *linear* encoding for autosegmental representations.

In a sense we have solved the problem already. Since the key autosegmental notions *tier* and *association* are now defined in terms of set-theoretic and arithmetic notions, we can utilize the well-understood

---

[5]The only part that cannot be reconstructed involves the simultaneous use of more than two tiers – this will be discussed in 1.5.

(and completely linear) notational systems of these disciplines to provide a linear encoding for autosegmental representations, although as we shall see in 1.4.1, there are some serious problems with this direct approach. In the light of these problems, 1.4.2 presents a set of criteria for evaluating linear encodings, and shows that no encoding system can meet these criteria fully. Thus we are forced to develop less than fully optimal encodings: the *scanning* code is presented in 1.4.3, and the *triple* code, due to Karttunen (pc), is described in 1.4.4. Some criticisms of these encodings and alternative proposals by Wiebe 1992 and Bird and Ellison 1994 are discussed in 1.4.5.

1.4.1   The mathematical code

It is easy to express autosegmental representations in a linear notation by using the standard mathematical notations for the ordered triples, relations, and functions that played a role in the formal definition of bistrings. But there are problems with this direct approach.

First, the resulting notation, though clearly linear, would be exceedingly cumbersome. While this is not a serious problem from a high-level theoretical perspective, there can be little doubt that the rapid spread of autosegmental theory was due largely to the fact that it provided a perspicuous notation for configurations such as floating tones or contours which are frequently encountered in linguistic practice and for which such notation was lacking. It cannot be realistically hoped that a formalism that uses the string $((f(x) = G, x \neq 0, 1; f(0) = H; f(1) = L), (g(x) = G, x \neq 0; g(0) = V), \{(0,0), (1,0)\})$ to denote the falling tone vowel that linguists depict as (1) above would be widely adopted, no matter how unambiguous or well-defined.

Second, the nature of the subject matter makes it highly unlikely that the mathematics that comes with these notations will be in any way relevant. In particular, the use of arithmetic in phonology is viewed with widespread (and in my opinion, totally justified) suspicion. The proper linear notation should be one that evokes a mathematical apparatus that was created with linguistic problems in mind, such as categorial grammar or formal language theory.

Third, the syntax of the standard mathematical notation is essentially context-free (requires matching parentheses of arbitrary depth), while there is reason to believe that phonology does not require more than the expressive power of regular languages (Johnson 1970). Since the generative power of autosegmental theory has not been investigated before, it is important not to pre-judge the issue by choosing a notation that makes matters more complex than they need be. As we shall see shortly, it is indeed possible to linearize autosegmental representations in such a way that the syntax of the resulting expressions is finite state.

These considerations suggest that we should abandon the direct approach and encode autosegmental representations by linear strings in a different manner. The problem is to find a *coding function* C such that for any autosegmental representation A, $C(A)$ is a string over some finite *code alphabet* V_k.[6] It is clear that the coding function provided by the direct approach is far from being ideal, but it is less clear what an ideal coding function would look like – we turn to this question next.

1.4.2   The optimal code

The set of coding functions that we could use is extremely wide. For instance, we could enumerate all autosegmental representations (since there are only countably many) in some arbitrary order, and use their number, e.g. in hexadecimal notation, as their linear code. The objections one could raise against this coding scheme are not exactly the same as the ones listed in 1.4.1 above, but it is clear that this coding scheme is no less objectionable than the previous one. Rather than arguing, on a case by case basis, that certain encoding functions are bad, let us consider some criteria for good coding schemes.

---

[6]The subscript k denotes the cardinality of the code alphabet. This is the only thing that really matters – the precise nature of the letters in the alphabet is immaterial.

Computability   Clearly, the only interesting coding schemes are those that can be used in practice: given an autosegmental representation A its code $C(A)$ must be effectively computable in a finite (preferably small) number of steps. The absolute minimum we should demand is that C must be *recursive* (computable by a Turing machine), but the weaker the model of computation we use the better. Ideally, the code should be computable by the weakest kind of computing machinery available, namely finite automata.

Invertibility   Coding schemes that assign the same code to different representations are of little practical interest; the absolute minimum we should demand is that C must be *invertible*, but the easier to invert the code the better. Ideally, every possible string in V_k^* should be subject to decoding – if not, we will need some syntactic checking of the code words.

Iconicity   Many coding schemes are designed to minimize the similarity between the input and the output; for cryptographic purposes the ideal code would be the maximally opaque one. Here the ideal code should be as close to the original as possible. In particular, changing the input minimally should result in a minimal change in the output. For maximal iconicity, the changes should be localized, so that making a change at some point should leave the code of remote parts intact.[7]

Compositionality   The final requirement, closely linked to the idea of iconicity, is that the ideal coding scheme must be compatible with the basic operation of concatenation: $A = A_0 A_1 \Rightarrow C(A) = C(A_0)C(A_1)$. In other words, if A is composed from A_0 and A_1, the code of A should be composed from the code of A_0 and the code of A_1. A weaker, but perhaps more realistic, requirement is to permit the introduction of some fixed

---

[7]Perhaps the most common encoding scheme that does not meet this requirement is the one used in computers to encode numbers: changing a single digit in the input will affect not only the bits corresponding to the digit in question but also the *parity bit*.

'syncategorematic' element in the code of the composite representation: $A = A_0 A_1 \Rightarrow C(A) = C(A_0)SC(A_1)$, where S is independent of the choice of A_i.

Unfortunately, it is impossible to construct a coding function that meets all the above requirements maximally. Let us suppose indirectly that C is such a function. Restricting C to those autosegmental representations that contain the same number of nodes, say n, on both tiers will yield a set of code words R_n over some V_k^*. Since the coding is iconic, autosegmental representations of the same length n must yield code words of the same length $m(n)$. Furthermore, compositionality demands that concatenating autosegmental representations of length n l times should yield a code word of length $m(nl) = lm(n)$ (homogeneity) and that concatenating autosegmental representations of length n_0 and n_1 should yield a code word of length $m(n_0 + n_1) = m(n_0) + m(n_1)$ (linearity).

Since iconicity demands that the shorter the representation the shorter the code, $m(n)$ must be a monotonic, homogeneous, and linear function of n. The only such functions are $m(n) = cn$ where c is a non-negative constant. Since code length must be an integer, we are interested only in those cases where cn is a positive integer at least for some (ideally, for all) n-s. Therefore, we must suppose $c = p/q$, with p, q natural numbers. In the Appendix (section 1.6) I will show that a_n, the number of autosegmental representations over n points, is asymptotically

(5) $$a_n \approx (6 + 4\sqrt{2})^n$$

Since the code is invertible, $|R_n| = a_n$. Furthermore, since the number of code words of length $m(n)$ is $k^{m(n)} = k^{\frac{p}{q}n}$, we have

(6) $$a_n = k^{\frac{p}{q}n}$$

Combining these we get

(7) $$k^{\frac{p}{q}n} \approx (6 + 4\sqrt{2})^n$$

But this would mean that

$$(8) \qquad\qquad k^{\frac{p}{q}} = (6 + 4\sqrt{2})$$

must hold for some positive integers k, p, q, which is impossible since if we raise both sides to the q-th power the left-hand side is an integer and the right-hand side is not.

In the Appendix, I will show that the problem cannot be solved by restricting our attention to proper or fully associated representations. "The optimal code" promised in the title above simply does not exist.

1.4.3 The scanning code

In the light of the non-existence result presented above we must re-evaluate the desiderata listed above. Shall we give up computability? Since the proof does not use the assumption of computability, it is clear that we would gain nothing by such a move. Shall we give up, or at least weaken, compositionality? A closer inspection of the proof reveals that we would gain nothing by doing so. If we permitted some syncategorematic substring S of length s, instead of the original homogeneity assumption $m(nl) = lm(n)$, we would have $m(nl) = lm(n) + (l - 1)s$ and instead of the original linearity assumption, we would have $m(n_0 + n_1) = m(n_0) + m(n_1) + s$. Asymptotically this would still yield $m(nl) \approx l(m(n) + s)$ meaning that instead of c we would have a larger (but still rational) constant $c + s$ and the proof would go through as before.

Thus we are forced to weaken one or both of the remaining assumptions: we must be content with a less than fully invertible code and/or with a less than fully iconic one. The code to be presented here is near-optimal in the sense that it violates invertibility, iconicity, and compositionality only minimally.[8] Instead of being fully invertible (one-to-one onto) it is

---

[8] In this context Carnap's notions of explication quoted in fn. 2 of section 0.3 above are very relevant. An 'optimal' code is not one that uses the least number of bits given some

invertible if correct (one-to-one into). In other words, only a subset R of the possibly codewords in V_k^* will correspond to some autosegmental representation, and everything outside R will be treated as syntactically ill-formed. The violation is minimal because the well-formedness of a putative codeword can be trivially tested (by finite automata). Instead of being fully iconic, it is iconic modulo finite transduction. And instead of being fully compositional, it is compositional for all those representations that are associated at both ends. We will informally discuss the extent of these limitations as we go along, and analyze their causes more rigorously in chapter 2.5.

In order to present the code in a systematic fashion, let us start with the simplest possible autosegmental representations given in (9):

(9A)   (9B)

We will encode (9A) by the number 1, and (9B) by the number 0. In addition to these, we will need two other symbols, t and b, corresponding to a *top move* or a *bottom move* of a basic *biautomaton* which is informally defined as follows. The biautomaton has two tapes (corresponding to the two tiers) and a reading head which "spans" both tiers. The head, when positioned over square **x** of the upper tape and square **y** of the lower tape, can read the following information:

(i) Is there a symbol in cell **x**, and, if so, what symbol?

(ii) Is there a symbol in cell **y**, and, if so, what symbol?

---

assumptions about the probability distribution of autosegmental representations, but one that meets the (admittedly inexact) criteria of success listed in 1.4.2 above.

(iii) Is there an association line between the symbol in **x** and the symbol in **y**?

(iv) Are there further association lines from **x** to some cell after **y**?

(v) Are there further association lines from **y** to some cell after **x**?

In chapter 2, we will endow such a machine with finite-state control and the ability to advance nondeterministically one or both tapes – the resulting machine will be a two-tape no-turn Turing-machine with the additional capacity to read the association lines. But here we will use the machine only as a **coder** to make the definition of the linear code simple. The idea is that in scanning a well-formed autosegmental representation we can define uniquely which tape(s) should move.

(10)   If there are no further symbols on either tape, the coder stops. If there are no further symbols on one tape, the other tape is advanced by one. If there are no further association lines from **x** and **y**, both tapes move one step to the right, if there are further association lines from **x**, only the bottom tape moves, and if there are further association lines from **y**, only the top tape moves, provided the move does not result in scanning G. (The case when there are further lines both from **x** and **y** cannot arise, since such lines would cross.)

The code is simply a record of the moves and the association lines found during these moves. For example, in the representations given in (11), the corresponding codes are as in (12):

(11A) (11B) (11C) (11D) (11E) (11F)

```
 x  x   x  x   x  x   x  x   x  x   x  x
   |        |     |  |    /       \
 x  x   x  x   x  x   x  x   x  x   x  x
```

(11G) (11H) (11I) (11J) (11K) (11L)

```
 x  x   x  x   x  x   x  x   x  x   x  x
 | /    \ |    | \    / |    | / |   | \ |
 x  x   x  x   x  x   x  x   x  x   x  x
```

(12A) (12B) (12C) (12D) (12E) (12F)
 00   10   01   11   0t1b0 0b1t0

(12G) (12H) (12I) (12J) (12K) (12L)
1t1b0 0b1t1 1b1t0 0t1b1 1t1b1 1b1t1

Scanning always starts at the leftmost positions. If these are associated, we write down 1, if not we write down 0. At this point, we move the tapes according to (10), and write down a t if we made a top move, a b if we made a bottom move, and nothing if we moved both tapes. We repeat this process until the coder stops; the resulting string of 0s, 1s, ts, and bs is the linear code of the representation.

Clearly, we need not assume that the top tape has the same length as the bottom tape – the linear code defined here will work for any possibly 'skewed' autosegmental representation. While the code violates iconicity inasmuch as representations of the same length will not correspond to codes of the same length, the violation is minimal once these skewed representations are also taken into account. The violation of compositionality stems from the fact that the autosegmental concatenation of representations such as (11E) and (11J) does not necessarily preserve the synchronization inherent in the parts. And as for the invertibility of the code, codes are ill-formed iff they

(13.1) do not start or end in a number, or

(13.2) letters are not separated by numbers, or

(13.3) contain the subsequence $t0^*b$ or $b0^*t$.

These requirements are trivial to check. All other codes will correspond to some well-formed autosegmental representation, for instance, *1t11010b1t10* to

(14)

```
x x x x x x x x
|/ /   /  |/
x x x x x x x
```

Note, however, that for a bistring A decomposed as $A = A_0 A_1$, $C(A) = C(A_0)C(A_1)$ will follow only if the last elements of A_0 and/or the first elements of A_1 are associated. The immediate reason for this is requirement (13.3) above: even if $C(A_0)$ does not contain $t0^*b$ (but ends in $t0^*$) and $C(A_1)$ does not contain or $t0^*b$ (but begins in 0^*b), their concatenation will contain the prohibited substring. The deeper reasons for this partial failure of compositionality will be discussed in the Appendix to chapter 2.

1.4.4   The triple code

The scanning code, as defined in 1.4.3 above, deals only with the pattern of autosegmental associations, and completely ignores the content of the tiers. The easiest way to extend the linear code so as to include the content of the tiers is to flank the 1-s and 0-s by the autosegments they associate. Thus, for

(15)

```
a k c d e f g h
|/ /   /  |/
H H L M H L M
```

we would have *a1Htk1Hc1Hd0Le1Mf0Hbf1Ltg1Lh0M*. This is somewhat redundant, since each spreading autosegment is repeated as many times as it spreads[9]. Karttunen (pc) developed a code based on the idea that the redundancy can be eliminated by denoting the spreading pattern in the code with the addition of one extra symbol '_' for 'spreading site'. In this code, the basic inventory presented in (9) above is extended the following way:

(16A)	(16B)	(16C)	(16D)	(16E)	(16F)
x	x	x	x	x	x
|		′|	′|	′	′
y	y	y	y	y	y
x1y	x01	x1_	_1y	x0_	_0y

The symbols ′ and ′ above denote the kind of situation in which the scanning proceeds by top or bottom move respectively. This can happen either because there is an association line present, or because there are no further features on the bottom (resp. top) tier.

    The triple code uses the idea that deviations from the regular scanning pattern, which were encoded by *t*s and *b*s in the scanning code, can be absorbed in the content part of the ordinary scanning pattern, which is composed of *x1y*s and *x0y*s. What was encoded by *tx1y* in the scanning

---

[9]In section 2.2.2 we will see that the redundancy is easily removed.

code will be denoted by *x1_* in the triple code, what was *tx0y* in the scanning code will be *x0_* in the triple code, and similarly what was encoded by *bx1y* in the scanning code will be denoted by *_1y* in the triple code, and what was *bx0y* in the scanning code will be *_0y* in the triple code. For example, the triple code of the bistring in (15) will be *a1H k1_ c1H d0L e1M f0h _1L g1_ h0M* (spaces added only for ease of reading).

This idea enables us to encode every bistring as a regular succession of *triples* composed of the symbols of the top alphabet (plus the symbol '_'), the 1 or 0 encoding the presence or absence of the association line, and the symbols of the bottom alphabet (plus the symbol '_'). If there are k symbols in the top alphabet and n symbols in the bottom alphabet, this requires $2(k+1)(n+1)$ triples. In the most typical case in autosegmental representations, the 'P' tier contains a binary feature ($k = 2$) and the 'P-bearing' tier contains archisegments ($n \approx 30$), so triple encoding requires some 186 symbols which at first sight compares unfavorably with the $n + k + 4 = 36$ symbols required by scanning encoding. But of course the triple encoding is at least two thirds shorter, so the economy of the scanning encoding is illusory.

Roughly speaking, the triple code is a fixed length code while the scanning code is variable length[10] – each has its advantages. If the association patterns are our primary object of study and the content of the tiers is less important, the scanning code is better as it uses only 4 symbols where the triple code uses 6. But if we are primarily interested in the content of the tiers, and the abstract pattern of associations is less important, the triple code is better because "fixed length" leads to automata with more transparently organized state space (see in particular 2.2.2).

---

[10]Strictly speaking this distinction does not make full sense as the bistrings that are encoded by these schemes have no obvious length measure.

1.4.5 Subsequent work

While the criteria proposed in 1.4.2 for the evaluation of linear encodings have met with the approval of researchers in the field, the same cannot be said about the scanning code presented in 1.4.3 or Karttunen's triple code presented in 1.4.4 above – both Wiebe 1992 and Bird and Ellison 1994 criticize these encodings and offer interesting alternatives. First, these authors note that the definition of the codes does not cover the cases when one or both tiers are empty. At least for the scanning code, which requires the coder to start on the first nonempty cells of each tier, this problem cannot be remedied without some *ad hoc* stipulations.

However, it is not clear whether this is a real drawback. Given that our formalization did not permit dangling association lines (see 1.3 above), the set of degenerate bistrings with the lower tier empty is isomorphic to the set of strings over the upper tier alphabet, which makes the whole issue of linearization moot. Further, as Wiebe's Theorem 4.3 demonstrates, no linearization extending to the degenerate cases can possibly be compositional, for, if it were, the codes of single symbols on the top tier would all have to commute with the codes of single symbols on the bottom tier (because the bistring-concatenation order of isolated symbols on separate tiers is immaterial), which in the free monoid over V_k is possible only if all these codes are powers of a fixed string c. However, such codewords would make the codes of non-commuting degenerate bistrings also commute, contradicting invertibility.

While Wiebe (1992:48-49) considers his result definitive, and opts for a k-tuple encoding of k-strings, it is worth emphasizing that his proof crucially depends on extending the code to the degenerate cases. From the perspective of the scanning and triple codes, Wiebe's Theorem 4.3 only demonstrates that fully compositional invertible linear codes cannot be so extended; it leaves the larger issues of iconicity and compositionality untouched. The methods of the Appendix (section 1.6) are asymptotic in nature, and therefore independent of what local tradeoffs one prefers for the simpler representations. Wiebe notes that degenerate representations such as tonal morphemes without segmental content and toneless morphemes coexist in many languages, but his proof crucially relies on compositionality for such *short* bistrings, while the domain where compositionality actually becomes indispensable contains only *long* bistrings for which a mere tabulation of codes becomes infeasible.

Autosegmental representations allow for two kinds of adjacency: elements on the same tier can be string-adjacent and elements on different tiers can be associated. Because these notions are to a large extent independent. in linear encodings, where only string-adjacency is directly available, there is always tension between maintaining the linear order of elements in the tiers and maintaining the association structure. With the nonlinear encodings preferred both by Wiebe and by Bird and Ellison, the source of this tension is removed, and tierwise concatenation of k-strings becomes directly codeable as componentwise concatenation of k-tuples. However, the technique of investigating (families of) k-string-languages by investigating their codes, which was the main reason for introducing linear encodings in the first place, is no longer available. One of the most controversial questions about Autosegmental Phonology is its generative capacity – both the present work and Bird and Ellison 1994 argue that AP is regular, while Wiebe 1992 takes the position that it is outside the regular domain. In chapter 2 we will see how the technique of linear encoding can shed light on this issue.

1.5   Hierarchical structure

The representations used in present-day phonology typically involve more than two tiers. This is because in the modern theory there is no such thing as a segmental tier: it is just a shorthand for the more correct representation in which the segments are specified in terms of features located on a number of different tiers. In such a situation, it is necessary to specify which pairs of tiers can contain associated nodes.

This information is stored in a graph, called the *geometry* of features (see also the discussion in section 4.1).

The trend in autosegmental phonology is to put more and more features on separate tiers: first tone (as in Leben 1973), then vowel features (such as ATR and Back) participating in vowel harmony (Clements 1976), laryngeal features (Thráinsson 1978), nasality (Hyman 1982), syllabicity (Clements and Keyser 1983 ch 3.8), etc. The logical endpoint of such a trend is a representation resembling a paddle wheel (Archangeli 1985:337), in which every feature is on a separate tier, and they are all linked to a central (root) tier. This proposal, also known as the **Independent Linking Hypothesis** (ILH) gives us a 'geometry' graph shaped as a star.

Another, more refined, proposal was put forth by Clements 1985: here the graph has a more complex tree structure. Different (rooted) tree structures were proposed by Sagey 1986, Schein and Steriade 1986, Archangeli and Pulleyblank 1989, Halle and Ladefoged 1988 and others – we will return to these proposals in section 4.1 and again in section 5.3. Without committing ourselves to the details of any of these proposals, let as define the **content** of a leaf node in the geometry as the feature labeling of the node in question, e.g. [+back], and the content of internal nodes, called **class nodes**, as the set of the contents of its daughters.

It follows from the definition that the content of the root node can take only a finite number of values. Ideally, the inventory of features and the geometry is chosen so that all these values are meaningful, but in practice certain combinations need not correspond to actual segments. The notion of featural content can be trivially generalized to deal with complex segments and partially assimilated clusters, because the complexity of such configurations is limited to features spanning one or two nodes.

While the notion of featural content would also generalize to the case of suprasegmental tiers where any element on one tier can have an arbitrary long melody associated to it, the idea of using segment-like (archiphonemic) abbreviations for nodes with a given content would not, because that would require an infinite number of symbols. This means that those representations in which there is more than one melodic tier (e.g. cases of vowel harmony with more than one harmonizing feature) cannot be linearized using a single bistring. There are two natural ways to deal with this problem: first, we can linearize every plane of the representation separately; second, we can extend the definition of the automaton described in section 1.4 so that the reading head can scan a full temporal slice of a multi-tiered representation. We will return to this issue in chapter 2.

In addition to the hierarchical structure provided by feature geometry, autosegmental representations can also have explicitly marked hierarchical structure. A full discussion of the constituent structure provided by metrical phonology is beyond the scope of this work – I will limit myself to non-recursive boundary symbols.[11] Aside from the blank spaces which are often used as a kind of typographically hidden parenthesis,[12] the most important delimiter in autosegmental phonology is the *long bracket* indicating the simultaneous beginning (or end) of two or more tiers. In addition to its obvious use in separating larger (at least morpheme-sized) constituents from one another, long brackets are used in three additional functions:

(17.1) Indicating the association domain of floating elements

(17.2) Fixing the location of certain features to the edge

(17.3) Supporting abstract features pertaining to the whole domain

(17.1) is perhaps the most typical use of long brackets: for example, compare the treatment of Tiv and Margi in Pulleyblank 1986. The use of boundary tones in Hyman 1982 is a good example of (17.2), while (17.3) is encountered mostly in connection with morphosyntactic features such as lexical category marking.

---

[11] As long as a relatively weak form of the Strict Layer Hypothesis (Nespor and Vogel 1986) can be maintained, this is not a real limitation.

[12] Cf. the provision in (10) that the automaton cannot "fall off" either tier.

The long brackets surrounding bistrings can be encoded by ordinary brackets surrounding the linear code of bistrings. This will work for 1. and 3. but not, without further conventions, for 2. Note that the linearization of long brackets is obviously iconic and compositional in the sense of section 1.4.

1.6 Appendix

In this section, I will first prove the asymptotic formula (5) for the number of autosegmental representations using the method of generating functions. Next I will establish a similar asymptotic result for fully associated autosegmental representations, and prove an exact result for the proportion of fully associated representations. Finally, I apply the method of generating functions to the case of proper autosegmental representations. For this case, no closed form asymptotics is given, but the key irrationality result, which makes the enumeration relevant for coding, is proved.

Let us denote by a_n the number of distinct association structures between two tiers, each containing a string of length n. Recall that $a_1 = 2$, $a_2 = 12$ (cf. (9) and (11) above). In general, the number of such structures with length n can be expressed recursively. Let us denote the number of well-formed structures with n points on the top row and k points on the bottom row by $f(n, k)$. By symmetry, $f(n, k) = f(k, n)$, and obviously $f(n, 1) = f(1, n) = 2^n$, since in such configurations there can be n association lines, and the presence or absence of any one of them is independent from the presence or absence of the others. With this notation, $a_n = f(n, n)$.

In a structure such as (18A), we can single out the first association line that runs from the bottom tier to the last x on the top tier.

```
(18A)
  1 2 ....... n n+1
  x x x x x x x x


  x x x x x x x
  1 2 ... i ..k+1
```

If this line runs from the ith bottom node to the $n + 1$st top node, we can decompose (18A) into the two parts given in (18B), and (18C).

```
(18B)                         (18C)
  1 2 ... i   ...n                      n+1
  x x x x x x x x                        x


  x x x x x                           x x x
  1 2 ... i                           i+1..k+1
```

The number of permissible configurations for (18B) is, by definition, $f(n, i)$, while the number of permissible configurations for (18C) is $f(1, k + 1 - i) = 2^{k+1-i}$ since, by the same reasoning as above, each of the association lines from x(n+1) in the top row to x(i+1), x(i+2),...x(k+1) in the bottom row can be chosen independently of the others. Therefore, we have

$$(19) \qquad f(n+1, k+1) = \sum_{i=1}^{k+1} f(n, i) 2^{k+1-i} + f(n, k+1)$$

The extra term $f(n, k + 1)$ counts the cases where the $n + 1$st node is not linked at all. The same equation for k one less is given under (20) in a form where both sides are multiplied by 2:

$$(20) \qquad 2f(n+1, k) = \sum_{i=1}^{k} f(n, i) 2^{k+1-i} + 2f(n, k)$$

Now, subtracting (20) from (19) gives (21):

(21) $$f(n+1, k+1) - 2f(n+1, k) =$$
$$f(n, k+1) + f(n, k+1) - 2f(n, k)$$

Rearranging the terms we have our basic recursion:

(22) $f(n+1, k+1) = 2f(n+1, k) + 2f(n, k+1) - 2f(n, k)$

Using this recursion the first few values of a_n can be computed as 2, 12, 104, 1008, 10272, 107712, 1150592, and so on. As can be seen, a_n is divisible by 2^n but not by any other power c^n for any integer c. For some readers, these few terms in the sequence will constitute sufficient evidence that there can be no 'perfect' linear encoding of autosegmental structures, since a perfect code using, say, d symbols would use all strings of length n for the encoding and thereby give rise to d^n structures. Readers not satisfied with this heuristic argument should read on.

Using (20) we can calculate backwards and define $f(0, n) = f(n, 0)$ to be 1 so as to preserve the recursion. The generating function

(23) $$F(z, w) = \sum_{i,j=0}^{\infty} f(i, j) z^i w^j$$

will therefore satisfy the equation

(24) $F(z, w) - 2zF(z, w) - 2wF(z, w) + 2zwF(z, w) =$
$$1 - z - w - z^2 - w^2 - \dots$$

Therefore, we have

(25) $$F(z, w) = \frac{1 - \frac{z}{1-z} - \frac{w}{1-w}}{1 - 2z - 2w + 2zw}$$

In order to see that the power series (23) actually converges, let us consider the following trivial upper bound. Since $f(1, k) = 2^k$, $f(n, k) < 4^{n+k}$ is initially satisfied, and by induction $f(n+1, k+1) = 2f(n+1, k) + 2f(n, k+1) - 2f(n, k) < 2 \cdot 2 \cdot 4^{n+k+1} = 4^{n+k+2}$. Therefore, if

$|z|, |w| < 1/4 - \epsilon$, say $1/5$, the series is absolutely convergent, and can be rearranged in any order. For our purposes we will actually rearrange it along the $i + j = n$ diagonals. If we substitute $w = t/z$ and consider the integral

(26)
$$\frac{1}{2\pi i} \int_C \frac{f(z, t/z)}{z} dz$$

over a contour C in the crown $1/25 < |z| < 1/5$ (keeping t fixed), this will yield the constant term $\sum_{n=0}^{\infty} f(n, n)t^n$ by Cauchy's formula. Therefore, in order to get the generating function

(27)
$$d(t) = \sum_{i=0}^{\infty} a_n t^n$$

we have to evaluate

(28)
$$\frac{1}{2\pi i} \int_C \frac{1 - \frac{z}{1-z} - \frac{t/z}{1-t/z}}{z(1 - 2z - 2t/z + 2t)} dz$$

This can be done by the method of residues. Since the denominator is quadratic, the poles can be located easily: $p, q = (2t + 1 \mp \sqrt{1 - 12t + 4t^2})/4$. In the first two terms of the numerator, the only pole near the origin is at p. Since it is simple, the residue is given by

(29)
$$\lim_{u \to p} (u - p) \frac{1 - \frac{u}{1-u}}{-2(u - p)(u - q)}$$

which gives

(30)
$$\frac{1 - \frac{p}{1-p}}{2(q - p)}$$

For the third term in the numerator we have to evaluate

(31)
$$\frac{t}{2\pi i} \int_C \frac{1/z}{2(z - p)(z - q)(1 - t/z)} dz$$

In addition to p, there is another simple pole in t so we get

(32)
$$\frac{t}{2(t - p)(t - q)} + \frac{t}{2(p - q)(p - t)}$$

Using $2(p+q) = 1 + 2t$, $2(q-p) = \sqrt{1 - 12t + 4t^2}$ we get

(33) $$d(t) = 1 + \frac{2t}{\sqrt{1 - 12t + 4t^2}}$$

$d(t)$ will thus have its first singularity when $\sqrt{1 - 12t + 4t^2}$ vanishes at $t_0 = (3 - \sqrt{8})/2$. This gives the asymptotics for a_n which we used in section 1.4:

(34) $$a_n \approx (6 + 4\sqrt{2})^n$$

The base 2 logarithm of this number, 3.5431066, measures how many bits of information a length one segment of a bistring will carry on the average. Finer asymptotics can be obtained by expanding $d(t)$ around this singularity, but for our purposes this constant is sufficient.

The numbers $f(i,j)$ and $a_n = f(n,n)$ count all well-formed autosegmental representations, including extremely 'disorderly' ones. Let us define $g(i,j)$ as the number of representations containing no unassociated (floating) elements, and b_n as $g(n,n)$. Representations on $n+1, k+1$ points now can be divided into three classes. Those in which the last points are only associated to one another are $g(n,k)$ in number. Those in which the node x(n+1) on the top tier is associated to x(k) on the bottom tier are $g(n+1,k)$ in number. Finally those in which the node x(k+1) on the bottom tier is associated to x(n+1) on the top tier are $g(n,k+1)$ in number. Therefore, the basic recursion analogous to (20) is

(35) $g(n+1, k+1) = g(n+1, k) + g(n, k+1) + g(n, k)$

Using this recursion the first few values of b_n can be computed as 1, 3, 13, 63, 321, 1683, 8989, and so on. Using (35) we can calculate backwards and define $g(0,0)$ to be 1 and $g(i,0) = g(0,i)$ to be 0 (for $i > 0$) so as to preserve the recursion. The generating function

(36) $$G(z, w) = \sum_{i,j=0}^{\infty} g(i,j) z^i w^j$$

will therefore satisfy the equation

(37) $G(z,w) - zG(z,w) - wG(z,w) - zwG(z,w) = 1 - z - w$

Therefore, we have

(38) $\qquad G(z,w) = \dfrac{1 - z - w}{1 - z - w - zw} = 1 + \dfrac{zw}{1 - z - w - zw}$

(This time, the convergence of the power series (36) is already guaranteed since $g(n,k) \leq f(n,k)$.) Again we substitute $w = t/z$ and consider the integral

(39) $\qquad \dfrac{1}{2\pi i}\displaystyle\int_C \dfrac{f(z,t/z)}{z} dz$

over a contour C in the crown $1/25 < |z| < 1/5$ (keeping t fixed), this will yield the constant term $\sum_{n=0}^{\infty} g(n,n)t^n$ by Cauchy's formula. Therefore, in order to get the generating function

(40) $$e(t) = \sum_{i=0}^{\infty} b_n t^n$$

we have to evaluate

(41) $$\dfrac{1}{2\pi i}\int_C \dfrac{1}{z} + \dfrac{t}{z(1 - z - t/z - t)} dz =$$
$$1 - \dfrac{t}{2\pi i}\int_C \dfrac{dz}{(z - p)(z - q)}$$

The denominator is again quadratic: the poles this time will be $p,q = (t - 1 \mp \sqrt{1 - 6t + t^2})/2$. Again, only p is within the contour C, so we have

(42) $$e(t) = 1 + \dfrac{t}{\sqrt{1 - 6t + t^2}}$$

Notice that

(43) $$e(2t) = 1 + \dfrac{2t}{\sqrt{1 - 6\cdot 2t + (2t)^2}} = d(t)$$

and thus

(44) $$\sum_{i=0}^{\infty} b_n(2t)^n = \sum_{i=0}^{\infty} a_n t^n$$

Since the functions $d(t)$ and $e(t)$ are analytic in a disk of radius $1/10$, the coefficients of their Taylor series are uniquely determined, and we can conclude

(45) $$b_n 2^n = a_n$$

meaning that the fully associated autosegmental representations over n points are only an exponentially vanishing fraction of all such representations. In terms of information content, the result means that fully associated bistrings of length n can be encoded using $n2.5431066$ bits – exactly one bit less per unit length than for arbitrary well-formed bistrings.

Note: I could not find a simple 'bijective' proof of (45). It remains a challenge to establish this striking result by direct combinatorial methods.

Let us finally turn to the case of *proper* representations (in the sense of 1.3). Denoting their number by $h(n, k)$ the generating function $H = H(z, w)$ will satisfy a functional equation

(46) $$H - zH - wH - 2zwH + zw^2H + z^2wH - z^2w^2H = r(z, w)$$

where $r(z, w)$ is rational. Using the same diagonalizing substitution $w = t/z$ we have to evaluate

(47) $$\frac{1}{2\pi i} \int_C \frac{s(z, t)}{z(1 - z - t/z - 2t + t^2/z + tz - t^2)} dz$$

Again, the denominator is quadratic in z, and the radius of convergence is determined by the roots of the discriminant

(48) $$(t^2 + 2t - 1)^2 - 4(t - 1)(t^2 - t) = t^4 + 10t^2 - 8t + 1$$

The smallest root of this equation, approximately 0.15516939, is irrational. This can be shown as follows. Suppose, indirectly, that p/q is a solution of (48), with p, q relative primes. We have

(49) $$(p/q)^4 + 10(p/q)^2 - 8(p/q) + 1 = 0$$

therefore

(50) $$p^4 + 10p^2q^2 - 8pq^3 + q^4 = 0$$

and thus

(51) $$(p^2 + q^2)^2 = 8pq(q^2 - pq)$$

Since the right hand side is divisible by 8, $p^2 + q^2$ must be divisible by 4. But this is possible only if both p and q are divisible by 2, which contradicts the indirect hypothesis.

Next we establish the crucial result that its reciprocal $\beta = 6.4445742..$ cannot be expressed in the form $k^{p/q}$, where k, p, q are integers. Let us consider the reciprocal polynomial $P = t^4 - 8t^3 + 10t^2 + 1$. P is irreducible over the rationals, since its roots are all irrational, and as we shall demonstrate presently, P cannot be expressed as the product of two irreducible quadratic polynomials.

By Eisenstein's theorem it is sufficient to check this for quadratic polynomials S and T with integer coefficients. Since the leading coefficient and the constant term in P are both 1, it is sufficient to check $S = t^2 + ut + 1$, $T = t^2 + vt + 1$ and $S = t^2 + ut - 1$, $T = t^2 + vt - 1$. The former would yield $u + v = -8$ from the cubic term and $u + v = 0$ from the linear term, while the latter would yield $u + v = 8$ from the cubic term and again $u + v = 0$ from the linear term, both a contradiction.

Therefore, P is irreducible over the rationals and if $\beta = k^{p/q}$ would hold then P would divide $t^q - k^p$:

(52) $$t^q - k^p =$$
$$(t^4 - 8t^3 + 10t^2 + 1)(r_0 t^{q-4} + r_1 t^{q-5} + ... + r_{q-5}t + r_{q-4})$$

Let us denote the quotient polynomial $t^{q-4} + r_1 t^{q-5} + ... + r_{q-3}t + r_{q-4}$ by $H(t)$. Differentiating both sides of (53) repeatedly and substituting $t = 0$ we get $r_{q-4} = -k^p, r_{q-5} = 0, r_{q-6} = 10k^p, r_{q-7} = -8k^p$ and in general

(53) $$0 = H^{(i)}(0) + 10i(i-1)H^{(i-2)}(0) -$$
$$8i(i-1)(i-2)H^{(i-3)}(0) + i(i-1)(i-2)(i-3)H^{(i-4)}(0).$$

From this we can prove by induction that $i!k^p$ will divide $H^{(i)}(0)$, and thus k^p will divide the leading coefficient r_0 of $H(t)$, contradiction.

The theorems proved above lead to the conclusion in 1.4.2 that no code can be fully invertible, iconic, and compositional. The codes presented in 1.4.3 and 1.4.4 are quite compositional and iconic, but invertible only for well-formed code strings. If we viewed full invertibility as the overriding optimality criterion, it is an open question whether reasonably compositional/iconic codes could still be found.

1.7   References

Archangeli, Diana 1985.   Yokuts harmony: evidence for coplanar representation in nonlinear phonology. *Linguistic Inquiry* **16** 335–372.

Archangeli, Diana and Douglas Pulleyblank 1989.   *The content and structure of phonological representations.* ms, forthcoming from MIT Press, Cambridge MA.

Bagemihl, Bruce 1989.   The crossing constraint and 'Backwards Languages'. *Natural Language and Linguistic Theory* **7** 481–549.

Bird, Steven and T. Mark Ellison 1994.   One-level phonology: autosegmental representations and rules as finite automata. *Computational Linguistics* **20** 1 .

Bird, Steven and Ewan Klein   1989.   Phonological Events, University of Edinburgh Centre for Cognitive Science, EUCCS/RP-24.

Bird, Steven and Ewan H. Klein 1990.   Phonological events. *Journal of Linguistics* **26** 33–56.

Chomsky, Noam and Morris Halle 1968.   *The Sound Pattern of English.* Harper & Row, New York.

Clements, George N. 1976.   Vowel harmony in nonlinear generative phonology. In *Phonologica*, Wolfgang U. Dressler and Oskar E. Pfeiffer, (eds.) Innsbruck.

Clements, George N. 1985. The geometry of phonological features. *Phonology Yearbook* **2** 225–252.

Clements, George N. and Kevin C. Ford 1979. Kikuyu Tone Shift and its Synchronic Consequences. *Linguistic Inquiry* **10** 179–210.

Clements, George N. and S. Jay Keyser 1983. *CV Phonology: A Generative Theory of the Syllable*. MIT Press, Cambridge.

Coleman, John and John Local 1991. The "No Crossing Constraint" in Autosegmental Phonology. *Linguistics and Philosophy* **14** 295–338.

Goldsmith, John A. 1976. *Autosegmental Phonology*. PhD Thesis, MIT.

Goldsmith, John A. 1990. *Autosegmental and metrical phonology*. Basil Blackwell, Cambridge MA.

Halle, Morris 1983. Distinctive features and their articulatory implementation. *Natural Language and Linguistic Theory* **1** 91–107.

Halle, Morris and Peter Ladefoged 1988. Some major features of the International Phonetic Alphabet. *Language* **64** 577–582.

Hyman, Larry M. 1982. The representation of nasality in Gokana. In *The Structure of Phonological Representation*, Harry van der Hulst and Norval Smith, (eds.) Foris, Dordrecht.

Johnson, Ch. Douglas 1970. *Formal aspects of phonological representation*. PhD Thesis, UC Berkeley.

Karttunen, Lauri pc. Personal communication.

Kornai, András 1989. A note on *Phonological Events*, ms, Stanford University.

Leben, William 1973. *Suprasegmental phonology*. PhD Thesis, MIT.

Leben, William R. 1978. The Representation of Tone. In *Tone: a Linguistic Survey*, Victoria Fromkin, (ed.) Academic Press, New York, 177–220.

Nespor, Marina and Irene Vogel 1986. *Prosodic phonology.* Foris, Dordrecht.

Pulleyblank, Douglas 1986. *Tone in lexical phonology.* D. Reidel, Dordrecht.

Sagey, Elisabeth 1988. On the ill-formedness of crossing association lines. *Linguistic Inquiry* **19** 109–119.

Sagey, Elizabeth 1986. *The representation of features and relations in non-linear phonology.* PhD Thesis, MIT.

Schein, Barry and Donca Steriade 1986. On geminates. *Linguistic Inquiry* **17** 691–744.

Scobbie, James M. 1991. *Attribute Value Phonology.* PhD Thesis, University of Edinburgh.

Stevens, Kenneth N. and Sheila E. Blumstein 1981. The search for invariant acoustic correlates of phonetic features. In *Perspectives on the study of speech*, P. Eimas and J. Miller, (eds.) Lawrence Erlebaum Associates, Hillsdale, NJ.

Thráinsson, Höskuldur 1978. On the phonology of Icelandic preaspiration. *Nordic Journal of Linguistics* **1** 3–54.

Wiebe, Bruce 1992. *Modelling autosegmental phonology with multitape finite state transducers.* MS Thesis, Simon Fraser University.

Chapter 2

Rules

In the previous chapter we have seen that autosegmental representations can be replaced by typographically less transparent, but informationally equivalent linear strings. Is autosegmental phonology just a typographical gimmick, or is there a substantive difference between the linear and the nonlinear systems? In order to answer this question, we have to go beyond the analysis of data structures and investigate the basic computational devices of phonological theory, called *autosegmental rules*.

Section 2.1 distinguishes *phonological* and *phonetic* rules and presents a variety of phonological rule ordering hypotheses from the perspective of *finite state control*. Section 2.2 discusses the major phonological rule types and exemplifies the method of encoding these in a linear fashion. Section 2.3 introduces a class of autosegmental automata that operate directly on autosegmental representations, and exemplifies the method of replacing phonological constraints and rules by such automata. The generalization of these results to multi-tiered representations is discussed in section 2.4.

The Appendix (section 2.5) develops the basic theory of autosegmental languages and automata, and provides several equivalent characterizations of *regularity* in this domain. Kleene's theorem is generalized to the autosegmental case. This generalization has some rather striking implications for the theory of autosegmental phonology, in particular for theories of reduplication and for a deeper understanding of Leben's (1973) Obligatory Contour Principle – these are discussed in 2.5.3.

2.1 Data and control

From the perspective of the speech engineer interested in the actual physical phenomenon of speech, phonological theory is primarily a method of data compression. Instead of having to deal with a large number of quickly changing continuous parameters, phonological theory promises to reduce the task to dealing with a small number of slowly changing discrete parameters. The price to be paid for this data compression[1] is that the parameters of the compressed representation, namely the features, are no longer directly interpretable in physical terms.

From the perspective of the phonologist, the relationship between the features and the physical parameters is conceptualized in terms of an uncompression, rather than in terms of a compression, algorithm. The elementary procedural steps of this algorithm, called *rules*, fall into two broad classes: rules of phonological derivation, and rules of phonetic interpretation. The *phonological* component of the grammar, which includes both lexical and postlexical phonology, takes morphemes and morphosyntactic features as its input, and provides a quite detailed phonemic representation for the well-formed words that it generates. The *phonetic* component of the grammar takes the output of the phonological component as its input, and provides an articulatory phonetic representation that will, in turn, give rise to an acoustic representation. Ignoring the internal (stratal) organization of the phonological component, and restricting our attention to segmental phonology, this can be depicted as follows:

---

[1] According to O'Shaughnessy 1987 Table 7.1, the bit-rate should be reduced from 96kbits/sec to 200bits/sec. Flanagan 1972 Ch.1.2 gives somewhat different figures (30kbits/sec vs. 50 bits/sec) but essentially the same ratio (5-6 hundredfold reduction).

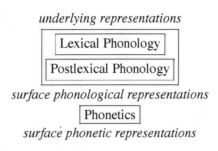

The justification for this division of labor is that phonology deals with the mental representation of sound, composed of discrete units such as syllables, phonemes, and features, while phonetics deals with the physical representation of sound which is, ultimately, continuous. Furthermore, the phonological rules that characterize the lexical component are arbitrary in the sense that rules other than those actually observed in a language would be just as possible, while the rules of phonetic realization can be motivated in the sense that they depend on the laws of physiology and acoustics. Phonological rules can vary a great deal in time, across languages and dialects, and are riddled with exceptions, while phonetic rules are more constant and admit no exceptions.

The rules relating underlying representations to surface representations are traditionally divided into three broad classes of *morphological, phonological* and *phonetic* rules (with the possible addition of a fourth class of *morphonological* rules, see e.g. Dressler 1985). The model-theoretic framework adopted here will make it necessary to follow this classification as far as the distinction between phonetic rules (envisioned here as rules of interpretation) and non-phonetic rules is concerned, but it is neutral with respect to the other traditional distinctions. In the present section I will abstract away from the actual inventory of phonological rules and concentrate on the way these rules interact in a derivation.

In SPE phonology (Chomsky and Halle 1968) the input and output specifications of phonological rules are called *structural Description* (SD) and *Structural Change* (SC), respectively – these terms are long familiar from transformational syntax (Chomsky 1957, Chomsky 1965). Given a form f and a rule r such that $a \cdot SD(r) \cdot b = f$, we say that $a \cdot SC(r) \cdot b = (f)r$ is the result[2] of applying r to f. In case $fr = f$ we say the rule *applied vacuously*. For the sake of completeness, we can define a result even in case the structural description of the rule r is *not* met by a form g. In this case we say that the rule applied with *appearance checking* and its output is $gr = g$ (see Salomaa 1973 Ch 6).

In the standard (linear) case, the rule of choice is context-sensitive rewriting, and '·' is the operation of concatenation, but the definition will work just as well for transformations, context-free rewrite rules, and nonlinear phonological rules. Given a set of rules $R = \{r_1, r_2, \ldots, r_n\}$, and a set of underlying forms $U = \{u_1, u_2, \ldots, u_k\}$ we can try to apply every rule to every form. This will yield the set $UR = \{u_i r_j | u_i \in U, r_j \in R\}$, to which we can again apply every rule, yielding UR^2 and so on. If we consider the totality of forms in $L = \cup_{i=0}^{\infty} UR^i$ (defining, as usual, UR^0 to be U), we get the notion of a language generated by a *pure grammar* (Maurer, Salomaa and Wood 1980). In syntax, U is usually taken to be a single start symbol S, and only those strings of L are considered which do not contain nonterminal symbols. In phonology, however, the set U contains the underlying form for every morpheme in the language, and the nonterminal/terminal distinction is seldom crucial.

In the field of phonology, the basic control structures are known as various types of *rule orderings*. Before turning to a discussion of more complex structures involving the cycle, the strict cycle, and stratal organization, let us first recapitulate some of the key results of Pelletier 1980 concerning rule ordering within a cyclic domain. Let us assign a set of labels T_i to each rule r_i. In the simplest case each set is a singleton and no two different productions have the same label. In this case we can use the subscripts $1, 2, \ldots, n$ themselves as labels. Each derivation yields a string of the labels, called the *control string*, and various hypotheses concerning rule ordering can be stated as restrictions on such control strings.

---

[2]I will use the algebraic notation placing the function on the right and the argument on the left. Parentheses will be omitted unless ambiguity threatens.

Total ordering means that a fixed permutation of the labels, say
123...n, is the only permitted control string, i.e. that the rules apply
in a given order. This hypothesis (also known as full linear extrinsic
ordering), is to be contrasted with an uncontrolled application of rules
(the random sequential hypothesis of Koutsoudas 1976) which yields all
the forms that can be derived from underlying forms by applying the
rules in some order. In this case the control language is $\{1, 2, ..., n\}^*$.
Iterative rule application, meaning that a rule can reapply to its own output
arbitrarily many times but cannot reapply to the output of later rules
(see Kenstowicz and Kisseberth 1973) would correspond to the control
language $1^+2^+...n^+$. The idea that rules can apply in any order, except
that a rule once applied is no longer eligible for application ('Principle
VI' of Ringen 1976) corresponds to $\{1, 2, ..., n\}^* \setminus \cup_{1 \leq i \leq n} \alpha i \beta i \gamma$.

As the readers can verify for themselves, the alternatives considered
by Pelletier (1980) can all be described with the aid of regular control
languages, and there are many other hypotheses that could also be described in this framework, most importantly, the overall hypothesis of
cyclic rule application.[3] Staying within a single cycle, Pelletier shows
that among the various hypotheses entertained by phonologists at one
time or another, total orderings have the smallest strong generative capacity and random orderings have the greatest, with iterative orderings
and 'Principle VI' being incomparable theories of intermediate strength.
Interestingly, total ordering has the same generative power as simultaneous rule application. The terminology can be a little confusing. While
random orderings are the 'strongest' in Pelletier's technical sense, what
this really means is that random ordering is the weakest hypothesis about
the class of languages generable under some ordering restriction, and total ordering is the strongest (most restrictive) hypothesis. In other words,
every language that can be generated by some rule system with some
linear ordering imposed on it has a strongly equivalent grammar given
by some other rule system that is randomly ordered, but not conversely.

---

[3]In order to describe the strict cycle and other notions crucial to Lexical Phonology, we
will need a somewhat different apparatus – I will return to this matter in section 2.2.5.

However, these results crucially depend on a subtle point concerning the locus of rule application. It is often the case that a form f that can be decomposed as $a \cdot SD(r) \cdot b$ can also be decomposed as $a' \cdot SD(r) \cdot b'$ so that the rule r can yield either $a \cdot SC(r) \cdot b$ or $a' \cdot SC(r) \cdot b'$. To give an example, if $r = a \rightarrow bc$ and $f = aba$, $(f)r$ can be $bcba$ or $abbc$. As Matthews 1963 shows, if context-sensitive rules are restricted to apply at the leftmost possible site, the generated language is always context-free. Even more strongly, if context-sensitive rules do not apply to their own output, the generated language is actually regular, as shown by Johnson 1970, Kaplan and Kay ms. Since this result, taken at face value, seems to contradict Pelletier's results, it is necessary to consider the effects of restrictions on the place of rule application (locus effects) and on the order of rule application (control effects) together.

In order to put Johnson's theorem in proper perspective, let us recall a classical result of Chomsky 1959 which guarantees that a context-free grammar will only generate a regular language if it is not self-embedding. Therefore, if we take a context-sensitive grammar with no self-embedding, Matthews' theorem will guarantee the context-freeness, and Chomsky's theorem will in turn guarantee the regularity of the generated language. The advantage of this indirect proof over Johnson's direct proof becomes clear if we consider the following strengthening of Matthews' theorem (due to Cannon 1975): in a phrase-structure grammar, if the number of non-leftmost rule applications between leftmost applications is bounded, the resulting language is context free. Therefore Johnson's results rely on the lack of self-embedding more crucially than on a strict left-to-right manner of rule application.

2.2 The rules of autosegmental phonology

For a smooth integration of autosegmental phonology with Markov Models, it is quite essential to establish the finite-stateness of the autosegmental component. This is not to say that probabilistic techniques cannot be extended to the domain of context-free grammars (Baker 1979) or even further (Schabes 1991), but such extensions bring with them a computational cost that makes the development of large-scale systems unlikely in the foreseeable future. Therefore, it is quite important to show that neither locus nor control effects increase the power of the phonological component beyond finite state. In this section I will make an inventory of rule-types used in contemporary autosegmental phonology, and investigate their interaction in greater detail. The key regularity result will then be based on the rather trivial observation that regular grammars with regular control will only generate regular languages.

According to the traditional view (clearly articulated in contemporary terms by Anderson 1992, Zwicky 1992) the lexicon is semantically driven. The aim of a derivation is to create a word-form that encodes, in addition to the meaning of the stem, all the morphosyntactic information, such as number or case marking, that is relevant for placing the word in syntactic context. On this view, both derivational and inflectional rules function as spell-out rules that supply the relevant morphological marking, and their phonological form, be it suffixation, reduplication, or some other operation, is largely epiphenomenal.

In contrast to this, the 'mainstream generative' view of the lexicon is based on the observation that in general the morphology and the phonology of languages is tightly interwoven. The influential theories of Lexical Phonology and Morphology (Kiparsky 1982) and Prosodic Morphology (McCarthy and Prince 1986) both aim at creating a unified theory that can handle all sorts of 'lexical' regularities in an essentially combinatorial manner. Lexical Phonology proposes a stratal organization in which phonological rules and morphological operations are controlled by the same 'level-ordered' structure, and Prosodic Morphology attempts to reduce the inventory of morphological operations to the single operation of concatenation.

Since the goal is to create a formalism compatible with a wide variety of approaches, it is best to investigate the inventory of rules that are are necessary for the phonological description of morphological operations from a theory-neutral perspective. Whenever we find a linguistic regularity that the 'lexicon' (i.e. the combined effects of phonology and morphology) has to account for, the autosegmental mechanisms employed in its description are taken to be part of the inventory of phonological operations developed here. Extralinguistic regularities, such as poetic meter or word games, will not be considered.

2.2.1   Association and delinking

Perhaps the simplest possible operations on autosegmental representations are **association** and **delinking**, formally defined as the addition (subtraction) of an association line to (from) an association relation. There are so many automatic assimilation and dissimilation processes to provide motivation for these operations that only a simple example is provided here. In Hungarian, an l will totally assimilate to a following y under various conditions (for a detailed discussion, see Vogel and Kenesei 1987) so that $l + y$ becomes yy. In autosegmental phonology, assimilation is treated as the *spreading* of the y to the preceding timing unit (X), meaning that the first association line and the segmental unit l are removed from (1A) and an association line is added from the first timing unit to y to yield a y associated to two timing units as in (1B):

(1A)   (1B)

In terms of the linear code developed in 1.4, neither the insertion nor the deletion of an association line can be uniformly described. In the simplest case, when **x** and **y** are corresponding features that bear no other association, it is simply a matter of changing $x0y$ to $x1y$ (for association)

or $x1y$ to $x0y$ (for delinking). However, if the representation is more complex, the rule will take a correspondingly more complex form. As an example, let us encode the rule of spreading an associated H tone to the following toneless syllable:

```
  H
 /:
S S
```

This will be encoded as $H1SbH0S \rightarrow H1SbH1S$ or, in standard context-sensitive notation $0 \rightarrow 1/H1SbH\_S$. As this example shows, the ordinary iterative use of spreading rules will create no self-embedding, and thus will not increase generative capacity beyond finite state.

2.2.2   Insertion and deletion

The **insertion** of a node n on a tier T containing the string $Gt_1t_2..t_nG$ after t_j means that the class of mappings F_k that take $k + i$ into t_i for $0 \leq i \leq n$ and to G if i is outside this range is replaced by the class of mappings that take $k + i$ into t_i for $0 \leq i \leq j$; $k + j + 1$ into n; $k + i + 1$ into t_i for $j < i \leq n$; and i to G if i is outside this range. (The cases where n is inserted before t_1 or even before the first G or after the last G can be defined analogously.)

Similarly, the **deletion** of a node t_j from a tier T containing the string $Gt_1t_2..t_nG$ means that the class of mappings F_k that take $k + i$ into t_i for $0 \leq i \leq n$ and i to G if i is outside this range is replaced by the class of mappings that take $k + i$ into t_i for $0 \leq i < j$; $k + i$ into t_{i+1} if $j \leq i \leq n$; and i into G if i is outside this range.

According to these definitions, the insertion of a new node on a tier does not create any new association lines and the deletion of a node will require the concomitant deletion of all association lines that linked it to other tiers in order to restore the well-formedness of the representation. There are three distinct approaches in dealing with this problem – I will call them *filtering, monitoring* and *wait-and-see.* Under the **filtering** approach, the deletion of a linked node creates a 'dangling' association line and the derivation is blocked because the representation is no longer well-formed. This approach, exemplified by the Linking Constraint of Hayes 1986, sanctions deletion rules only to the extent that they explicitly take care of the association lines as well. Under the **monitoring** approach, exemplified by the Wellformedness Conventions of Clements and Ford 1979, there are a number of 'monitoring devices' in the background of any derivation that will slightly change the intermediate ill-formed representations in order to restore their wellformedness, in this case, by the deletion of any dangling association line. Finally, the **wait-and-see** approach would leave the representation ill-formed in the hope that some later rule will restore its well-formedness (at the end of the derivation we would still have a choice between filtering and monitoring).

The choice between these approaches is especially relevant when the inserted/deleted autosegment is a timing slot, because these are arguably governed by prosodic considerations such as the well-formedness of the resulting syllables (see in particular Itô 1989). The mechanisms of prosodic theory will be discussed in 2.2.4; here I restrict myself to the cases where insertion/deletion of an autosegment is governed by rule. In the linear code, insertion and deletion of nodes correspond to the insertion or deletion of code segments. For example, inserting a node y in

```
x  z
|  |
S  S
```

so as to yield

```
x  y  z
|    /
S  S
```

corresponds to $x1Sz1S \rightarrow x1Sy0Stz1S$ or, in standard context-sensitive notation, $0 \rightarrow y0St/x1S\_z1S$. Furthermore, the synchronization of the tiers might change, resulting in global changes in the code, as in the deletion of **y** from

x y z v w

X Y Z V W

which yields $x0Xz0Yv0Zw0Vbw0W$ from $x0Xy0Yz0Zv0Vw0W$. However, the changes always involve adjacent triples, so they can still be handled by finite transducers in spite of the fact that these are commonly thought of as being 'memoryless'. While it is certainly true that finite state devices cannot handle tasks that require an arbitrary amount of memory, it is perhaps worth emphasizing that they can in fact handle tasks requiring an arbitrary *but fixed* amount of memory. In the case of autosegmental representations, any version of the theory will use only a certain *fixed* and finite inventory of features (or feature:value pairs), and these can be encoded in the states of the machine.

To give a concrete example, let us see how the redundancy can be removed from the linear code. As we have seen at the end of chapter 1.4, a code word such as $a1Htk1Hc1Hd0Le1Mf0Hbf1Ltg1Lh0M$ is redundant for the representation

```
a k c d e f g h
|/ /   /  |/
H H L M H L M
```

because each spreading autosegment is repeated as many times as it spreads. Therefore the automaton that removes the redundancy will have to keep 'in memory' the last letter adjacent to a 1, and compare it to the next letter flanking the next 1 (if there is one) on the same side. To do this, we will need an n by k array of states, where n is the cardinality of the top tier alphabet and k is the cardinality of the bottom tier alphabet. For the sake of determinism, this array will be enlarged by a zeroth row and column, and triplicated in a third dimension, so that a single state can be described by a triple (u, v, x) where u is an element of the top tier alphabet (or 0), v is an element of the bottom tier alphabet (or 0), and x is 0, t, or b.

Let the starting state of the machine be (0,0,0). Upon encountering the first symbol u of the code (which will necessarily be a member of the top alphabet) the machine moves to state $(u, 0, 0)$ and outputs u. If the next symbol is a 0, the machine stays in $(u, 0, 0)$ (and outputs the 0); if it is 1, the machine moves to $(u, 0, t)$ (and outputs the 1). Next we get a symbol v from the bottom alphabet, which will be output, and the machine moves to (u, v, t) from $(u, 0, t)$ and stays in $(u, 0, 0)$ if it was in any $(x, y, 0)$ state (if there was no association line, there will be no redundancy to remove). At this point the machine can encounter a t or b symbol, which points to spreading (redundancy in the code) or it can encounter some element from the top alphabet, which means no spreading (no redundancy). In the case of no redundancy, the machine falls back to state $(u', 0, 0)$, where u' was the newly encountered element of the top alphabet, and outputs u'. But if there is redundancy, the state will remain (u, v, t) if a t was encountered, and will become (u, v, b) if a b is encountered (and the t or b is output).

The point of all this manipulation is to define a state space that will serve as a 'memory' storing the features linked by the last association line. Let us suppose that the machine is in state (u, v, t). If the next symbol encountered is u', this means that the v is spreading. The machine outputs the u' and moves into (u', v, t). At this point, it will of necessity encounter a 1, which is output, and will then encounter a v, which is *not* output. If the machine was in state (u, v, b), the same method is applied – the first u is not output but the 1 that necessarily follows it is output. This method will therefore remove the redundancy inherent in the repetition of labels (the dual transducer that puts it back is left as an exercise to the reader) in a way that is very close to the idea behind the triple-based encoding presented in 1.4.4 above. The 0th row and column can be thought of as corresponding to the symbol '_'.

Neither this transduction, nor triple-based encoding (which, by our preceding remarks, is essentially the same as building the transduction directly into the encoding) will remove the redundancy inherent in the fact that sequences of the form $tu0vb$ or $bu0vt$ are necessarily ill-formed[4] (cannot correspond to autosegmental representations). This is not to say that the redundancy inherent in the encoding of the association pattern cannot be removed – in fact as much of it can be removed as we wish, at the price of increased complexity of computation, and loss of iconicity in the code string. However, the redundancy in the encoding of the association pattern is so small that from a practical standpoint there is not much reason to eliminate it.

2.2.3   Concatenation and tier conflation

In defining the concatenation of bistrings in 1.3 above, I supposed that we concatenate the tiers with the same names (and tier alphabets) in a pairwise fashion quite automatically. However, the normal assumption in phonology is that concatenation will be more or less automatic only for one distinguished tier (the timing tier) and bringing all other tiers into alignment requires a separate operation, namely *tier conflation*. In fact, it would be possible to decompose tier conflation into conceptually even more simple micro-operations, such as 'finding the rightmost member on the segmental tier of the first morpheme', 'finding the leftmost member on the segmental tier of the second morpheme' and 'bringing these two into alignment'. But these putative operations seem to act in concert all the time, while with pure concatenation and tier-conflation this is arguably not the case, as we have to order other operations between them (see e.g. Cole 1987).[5]

While the notions of planar segregation and tier conflation are intimately linked to ideas of templatic morphology (see McCarthy 1989

---

[4]In the triple code, the analogous sequences are x0_ _0y and _0y x0_ .

[5]In a multi-tiered representation it is a further issue whether we must conflate all the tiers at the same time or whether we can, say, conflate the place tiers but leave the manner tiers separate until later.

for the connection and see McCarthy 1979 for the original statement of templatic morphology), for expository convenience I will present a simple example of tier conflation devoid of the templatic complexities to be discussed in 2.2.4 below. The reader should be aware that the example does not fully reflect the current phonological practice of using word-domain marking (see 2.2.5 below), rather than tier conflation, to handle phenomena of this sort, and that the data are considerably simplified.[6]

In Hungarian (and in most languages with vowel harmony), the domain of vowel harmony includes stems and suffixes, but not prefixes or compound stems. Traditionally, these facts are described by ordering prefixation and compounding after the rules of vowel harmony. The main problem with this otherwise straightforward solution is that it assigns the wrong internal structure to suffixed compounds. Rather then the semantically correct [[A B] S] they appear as [A [B S]]. This is particularly clear if the compounds in question are left-headed, such as *betűtípus* 'font' or *gabonaféle* 'cereal', which do not inherit the harmonic behavior of their heads *betű* 'letter' and *gabona* 'grain'.

Autosegmental phonology, by placing the harmonizing feature on a separate tier, offers a way out of this 'bracketing paradox'. The domain of harmony is defined as stem+suffix, but the morphemes of the compound stem appear on different planes[7] initially. Simplifying matters somewhat (for a more detailed discussion, see Kornai 1994), the basic rule of vowel harmony requires that stems with back vowels take the back alternant of suffixes such as the dative *nak/nek* and stems with front vowels take the front alternant so we get *fának* 'wood-DAT' but *fejnek* 'head-DAT'. In compounds, the second member is decisive, so we get *fejfának* 'grave-marker (lit. head-tree) -DAT' vs. *fafejnek* 'blockhead (lit. wooden-head) -DAT' rather than **fejfánek* or **fafejnak*.

---

[6]For the standard analysis of the phenomenon see Vágó 1980; for autosegmental treatments see e.g. Farkas and Beddor 1987, van der Hulst 1988.

[7]Following Archangeli 1985 I often speak of two tiers that can be connected by association lines as a *plane*. In our terminology every bistring can be located on one plane and one plane only.

As long as both kinds of stems have a feature associated to them at the relevant stage of the derivation, it makes no difference whether we use the unconflated representation

(2)

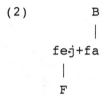

or the conflated representation

(3)   F   B
         | |
       fej+fa

because the spreading of the F[ront] autosegment would be blocked under both accounts: in (2) because it is in the wrong plane and in (3) because of the No Crossing Constraint. However, the difference becomes crucial when we introduce a third class of stems that contain *transparent* vowels. In Hungarian, the vowel *i* is generally transparent (for more details, see Ringen and Kontra 1989), so the choice of suffix is governed by the preceding vowel, as in *zafírnak* 'sapphire-DAT' and *zefírnek* 'zephyr-DAT'. This behavior is best captured by leaving the transparent vowel unassociated:

(4)   B   F
         | |
       zafirnAk   zefirnAk

Now, if a conflated representation of compounds such as (3) were in effect, the case in which the first member of the compound is B[ack] would similarly lead to back suffixation:

(5)   B
         |
       borviznAk

i.e. from *borvíz* 'mineral water (lit. wine-water)' we would get **borvíznak*
rather than the correct *borvíznek*, hence the need for the unconflated representation given in (2).

As this example shows, the intended effect of leaving the tiers unconflated is to block spreading. Formally, this will be encoded by a vertical
bar '|' to be placed between the linear encodings of the two bistrings that
make up the unconflated representation. The operation of tier conflation
corresponds to the deletion of this | which yields the simple concatenation
of the bistrings.

2.2.4   Templatic and Prosodic Morphology

With the aid of the phonological operations discussed so far it is impossible to describe the way reduplication is used to express morphological
categories (typically plurality or augmentation, but often less iconically
reduplicative categories such as tense or aspect). Each of the autosegmental accounts of reduplication involve one or more operations that fall
outside the inventory of operations discussed so far. Marantz 1982 uses
melody copy, *phoneme driven association*, and *floating element drop* in
addition to concatenation and tier-conflation, and only the last one of these
(also known as *stray erasure*) seems to be an independently motivated
phonological operation, comparable to association and delinking. In addition to stray erasure, Clements 1985a requires *transfer* and *sequencing*,
an operation that, as McCarthy and Prince 1986 argue, cannot be replaced
by the tier conflation operation discussed in 2.2.3 above. While the theory
developed in Mester 1986 uses no transfer, the sequencing operation is
still required. Finally, McCarthy and Prince 1986 require a weakening
of the No Crossing Constraint – an approach that changes the nature of
autosegmental phonology quite radically.[8]

Rather than providing a formalization for each or even most of these
approaches to reduplication, I will concentrate on the key mechanisms
employed by Prosodic Morphology (McCarthy and Prince 1986), namely,

---

[8]For an even more radical proposal along these lines, see Bagemihl 1989.

template satisfaction and *prosodic circumscription*, because these seem to be applicable to a wider range of phenomena that includes, besides reduplication and infixation, truncation as well (Mester 1990). For template satisfaction, my starting point will be Kiparsky 1987, where reduplication is analyzed so as to preserve the formal apparatus of templatic morphology, though the following discussion is more general inasmuch as it also makes provisions for the use of X units common to other analyses but not used by Kiparsky (1987).

For the sake of simplicity, let us define a (CV) *template* as a string of C,V, and X symbols, and a (phoneme) *melody* as a string over an alphabet which is exhaustively partitioned into two (not necessarily disjoint) nonempty subsets called c̲onsonants and v̲owels. Under this conception, each melody has its *Inherent Skeleton* which is defined by the following length-preserving homomorphism IS: if a phoneme p belongs in the consonant but not the vowel partition, $IS(p)=C$; if it belongs to the vowel, but not the consonant partition, $IS(p)=V$; and if it belongs to both partitions, $IS(p)=X$. The symbol X is usually conceptualized as a variable that can be instantiated either as C or as V. To reproduce this notion without introducing variables let us define the *nondeterministic* homomorphic mapping H which maps C to C, V to V, and X to either C or V.

A melody α will *perfectly satisfy* a template T if $IS(\alpha)=T$ or if $IS(\alpha)$ = H(T); i.e. if vowels match Vs, consonants match Cs, and phonemes of either type match Xs. The operational character of template satisfaction is not evident in such cases, because nothing really needs to be done to create a match – just aligning the template and the melody on parallel tiers and associating them one to one, left to right (or right to left) will create the expected bistring. However, if the template is shorter than the melody, some portion of the melodic material must get deleted (stray erasure) and if the melody is shorter than the template, multi-attachments will be created. Since any given template is finite, it is possible to create a template-specific finite transducer that will for any melodic input return a bistring describing the maximally satisfied template. However, there is no single finite transducer that will instantiate e.g. the principles of "template-driven association with priority for vowels" for such a transducer would require, in addition to the usual output tape, *two* input tapes: one for the melody and one for the skeleton. The natural way of describing the general mechanism of template satisfaction is with autosegmental automata – see section 2.3.

For **prosodic circumscription** my basic source will be McCarthy and Prince 1990, where the Arabic 'broken plural' is analyzed in depth. The fundamental idea of prosodic circumscription is that rules do not necessarily operate on morphologically defined units such as stems or roots, but can sometimes select a prosodically defined unit such as the syllable or the foot as their domain. In such cases, the rule that is prosodically circumscribed performs three separate tasks:

(i) Parse the morphologically defined base into a prosodic constituent unit (by definition located at the left or right edge of the base) plus a remainder, if any

(ii) Perform the rule on the prosodic unit (or on the remainder, depending on the specification of the rule)

(iii) Put the the result back together (or "unparse") with the remainder (or the original unit, if the operation was performed on the remainder) in the same order as they were before the parse

For example, in the formation of the Arabic broken plural a stem such as *jundub* will undergo the following changes:

(i) Parsing into a leftmost heavy syllable *jun* plus a remainder *dub*

(ii) A rule yielding *jVnVV* from *jun* is performed

(iii) The result *jVnVV* is put back together with the remainder *dub* to yield *jVnVVdub*

If prosodically circumscribed rules are composed in a parse$_1$, apply$_1$, unparse$_1$, parse$_2$, apply$_2$, unparse$_2$, ... sequence, the formal reconstruction of prosodic circumscription requires only the reconstruction of the suboperations of parsing, application, and unparsing. This can be trivially done by inserting, and later deleting, temporary boundary markers. Since these operations can all be modeled by finite state transductions, our basic conclusion that phonology is regular is unaffected by this mode of prosodic circumscription.

A more challenging case is when the prosodically circumscribed rules are not cascaded but *nested* in a sequence such as parse$_1$, apply$_1$, parse$_2$, apply$_2$, unparse$_2$, unparse$_1$. At first sight, this appears to be a case of context-free, rather than finite state control structure, given the lack of principled limitations on the depth of such nesting. But a closer look at the situation will reveal that the "matching parenthesis" effect is illusory. In any given grammar there will be only finitely many rules, and these can only create a finite depth of nesting.

Since this problem already came up once in our discussion of redundancy removal in 2.2.2 above, and will come up again in the discussion of reduplication in 2.5.3, it is perhaps worth calling this the *memorylessness fallacy*. Simply put, the reason why finite automata cannot handle context free languages is to be found in their memory limitations. If we can encounter matching parentheses of arbitrary depth[9] as we scan a string we need an arbitrary amount of memory, e.g. the kind provided by a pushdown store, to keep track of how many of these parentheses are still open. This reasoning will of course break down if we can put some fixed limit on the depth of the nesting or whatever information needs to be stored.

The memorylessness fallacy is based on a confusion between a structured class of problems and an unstructured collection of problems. To

---

[9]An important theorem of Chomsky 1962 asserts that every context free language is the homomorphic image of the intersection of a regular language and a Dyck language (language of matching parentheses), so we can restrict our attention to these.

give an example, suppose the problem is to find the roots of polynomials. When viewed as a structured class of problems, the only good solution is a general-purpose algorithm that takes polynomials as input and produces their roots as output. But when viewed as an unstructured collection of problems, we do not need a general-purpose solution. For each polynomial we are free to devise a separate root-finding algorithm that can exploit the specific properties of the polynomial in question.

In the case at hand, the problem is to express complex phonological operations, such as (prosodically circumscribed) template satisfaction by means of finite state devices. When viewed as a structured class of problems, there is no general-purpose finite state solution, for that would indeed require arbitrarily large amounts of memory. However, when viewed as an unstructured collection of problems, each of these can receive a finite state solution. We do not have a general-purpose finite state solution to the problem of recognizing strings in Dyck languages, so we do not have a general-purpose algorithm for modeling nested prosodically circumscribed rules by means of finite state control. But if we know that we need only a finite class of such strings recognized, we can of course devise a finite automaton for that class of strings, meaning that for any arbitrary but fixed grammar we can devise a special-purpose finite state model.

2.2.5 Domain marking

The marking of certain substructures as belonging to a certain prosodic domain such as the mora, syllable, foot, or (prosodic) word, or to a certain morphological domain such as root, stem, or (syntactic) word, is an essential part of phonological representations. First of all, a great number of phonological rules makes reference to such domains (for the syllable (in English) see Kahn 1976, for the foot (in Japanese) see Poser 1990, and for the morpheme (in Arabic) see McCarthy 1981), and at least one domain, the word, has been built into the very architecture of the theory. Second of all, domains in themselves can carry feature information –

boundary tones provide a clear and widely attested example. Third, and perhaps most important, is the existence of information that has to be associated with all the material in a domain, rather than with a selected part of it (e.g. with the nucleus of a syllable, or the left edge of a phrase). The most trivial example of this kind is *word meaning*, which has to be associated to the whole word, rather than to some part of it.[10]

The usual assumption in present-day phonology/morphology is that domain information is represented by hierarchical structure, rather than boundary markers. A typical example is the 'syllable tier' that contains a node for each syllable in a given string. Hierarchical structure can be represented both by trees or by a suitable 'geometry' of strictly tier-based structures – both methods are used widely in actual phonological practice. The operation naturally associated with tree structures is *percolation*, (see e.g. Lieber 1981, Selkirk 1982, while the operation naturally associated with 'geometry' is *projection* (see Halle and Vergnaud 1987). Of the two, percolation is problematic for the formalization developed here, as its most natural statement is within the context-free domain, along the lines of Knuth 1968. Projection, however, can be easily handled with the aid of (length-decreasing) homomorphisms, so it fits into the regular framework without any problem.

Thus we see two ways context-freeness can enter into the otherwise regular framework: via arboreal metrical structure or via morphological constituent structure. Since the necessity of arboreal metrical structure is highly questionable[11] the main source of non-finite-stateness that we have to deal with is morphological structure. Even here, affixation can usually be resolved without recourse to arbitrary depth matching parentheses, and only compounding requires genuinely non-regular structure (see Carden 1983, Culy 1985).

---

[10]While it is tempting to develop a 'purely syntactic' theory of the lexicon in which meanings play no part whatsoever, it should be kept in mind that such a theory will not be able to accommodate central insights of morphological theory such as *blocking* (see Aronoff 1976).

[11] See Prince 1983, Selkirk 1984 for arguments supporting this view, and Hayes 1984, Kager and Visch 1988 for arguments against it.

Though we succeeded in isolating the problem, it must be admitted that we did not really solve it, and that in fact there seems to be no solution that does not rely on some *ad hoc* stipulation. How seriously is the finite state approach compromised by its failure to handle hierarchical structure? At one extreme we find the view that hierarchical bracketing is at the heart of the cyclic mode of rule application, so that the phenomena handled by Lexical Phonology are by definition outside the purview of finite state machinery. At the other extreme we find the view that hierarchical structure of arbitrary depth is by no means the only way to deal with the most important phenomena, and that in fact grammarians can get by with a few nonrecursive boundary symbols that will give rise only to structures of limited depth.

From the internal perspective of phonological theory, the first view is better supported. Hierarchical structure has displaced boundary symbols in the vast majority of current phonological work. But from the external perspective imposed by the demands of applications, the second view makes more sense. The reason for this is that in the theory we are interested in the types, while in applied work we are interested in the tokens. For example, in the domain of stress assignment, which provides the strongest arguments in favor of hierarchical structure of unbounded depth, theoretical work is to a considerable extent driven by extremely long polysyllabic stems and compounds. But Zipf's law guarantees that these will appear extremely infrequently, so simple finite state models that fail to cover them can still be preferable to context-free or even more complex models that have only marginally[12] better coverage.

2.3 Automata

So far we have seen that the reconstruction of phonological analyses involves the manipulation of autosegmental representations (chapter 1) by autosegmental rules (section 2.2) subject to finite state control (section

---

[12]We will return to the issue of evaluating systems at the margin in section 5.4.

2.1). To complete this picture, we need to express the rules in terms of better understood data manipulation devices, namely, *automata*. Since in section 1.4 we provided encoding schemes that turn autosegmental representations into linear strings, it is now possible to express the autosegmental rules in terms of automata that manipulate these strings. However, there are some subtle issues concerning the expressive power of autosegmental rules that are blurred by this encoding procedure (for a full discussion, see the Appendix), so it is better to devise automata that operate directly on autosegmental representations.

In 2.3.1 one class of such devices, called *biautomata*, is introduced in lieu of the mathematically more appropriate, but for expository purposes more cumbersome class of *regular* autosegmental automata presented in the Appendix. Biautomata are then used for the explication of Tone Mapping (section 2.3.2), vowel projections (section 2.3.3), and reduplicative templates (section 2.3.4). Finally in 2.3.5 we answer the question posed at the beginning of this chapter: is autosegmental theory just a typographical gimmick?

2.3.1 Biautomata

In order to define devices manipulating autosegmental representations, it is instructive to consider devices manipulating simpler data structures such as strings. There is a wide variety of string manipulating devices in practical use, ranging from compression algorithms and stream editors to compilers and machine translation algorithms. From a theoretical perspective, they range from the simplest, called a *finite state transducer* or fst, to the most complex, such as a Turing-machine. Our aim here is to explicate autosegmental phonology in the simplest possible terms, so we will attempt to borrow as many features of fsts as we can.

A **finite state transducer**, as standardly defined, has an *input tape*, which it can only scan, and an *output tape*, which it can only write. Depending on its present state and the input symbol under scan, the fst writes one or more symbols on the output tape, advances the input tape, and moves into another state (possibly the same state). It is often convenient to modify this definition in such a manner that no writing takes place, the automaton can only scan both tapes, and will accept or reject any pair of tapes. With ordinary transducers, it does not matter at all whether the machine can write the tape or only reads it, the sets generated by writing are the same as the sets accepted by scanning. As we shall see, the same holds for autosegmental representations. There is no particular need to associate previously unassociated elements (or to delete an association line) as long as we can check whether a given association line appears and are free to reject the whole representation if it does not.

At any given state, a (read-only) fst can advance one of the tapes (and make an e-move on the other one), the other tape, both or neither (which gives it nondeterministic power). If we collect the pairs of letters that were under scan simultaneously, the collection will be a proper association relation assuming, as usual, that the machine can never go back to a position previously scanned. The resulting bistring can be called the *trace* of the program executed by the transducer. Such traces would therefore provide a method of defining bistrings and bilanguages using more or less standard transducers, but only for proper bistrings and bilanguages. Since not all linguistically relevant autosegmental representations are proper before a projection is taken, the automaton to be described below treats the association relation as part of the input data, rather than as a by-product of the scanning process.

Let us define **biautomata** as 6-tuples (S, T, U, i, F, t) where S is a set of states, T and U are the alphabets of the two tapes, i is the initial state, F is the set of final (accepting) states, and t is the *transition function* which, depending on the present state, the letters under scan, and the presence of association lines to these letters, will assign a new state, and advance the tapes (independently) by zero or one cell in accordance with the rule described in (10) in chapter 1. According to this definition biautomata are deterministic, since they must advance at least one tape.

From a linguistic perspective, deterministic automata are of great interest, since one of the tapes is often interpreted as containing timing units, and real-time operation means that on that tape the automaton will always have to advance. But from a mathematical perspective, *finite autosegmental automata* (which will not always advance automatically – see the Appendix for details) are closer to the "regular" family inasmuch as Kleene's theorem and the so-called finite index property hold for bilanguages accepted by regular autosegmental automata but fail for bilanguages accepted by biautomata. In the rest of section 2.3 I will use biautomata for the explication of phonological rules and constraints of various sorts. The question whether these can also be explicated in terms of regular autosegmental automata will be considered (and answered in the affirmative) in the Appendix.

2.3.2 Tone Mapping

As our first example of expressing phonological regularities by means of automata, let us consider the biautomaton that performs *Tone Mapping* in the sense of Williams 1976. **Tone Mapping** means association of P-bearing units and P-elements (syllables and tones) in a left to right, one to one manner, unless we run out of syllables, in which case tones remain unassociated, or run out of tones, in which case the last one spreads on the remaining syllables. The automaton to be defined here does not actually add any association lines – it simply checks the representation to determine whether the association lines are present in the manner predicted by Tone Mapping.

The finite state control of the automaton has only one state, the starting state. Upon encountering a singly associated tone associated with a singly associated syllable, the automaton remains in this state and both tapes are advanced simultaneously in accordance with the rule of automatic advancement given in (7) in chapter 1 and repeated here for convenience:

(1:10)   If there are no further symbols on either tape, the coder
          stops. If there are no further symbols on one tape, the other
          tape is advanced by one. If there are no further association
          lines from **x** and **y**, both tapes move one step to the right,
          if there are further association lines from **x**, only the bottom
          tape moves, and if there are further association lines from **y**,
          only the top tape moves, provided the move does not result
          in scanning G. (The case when there are further lines both
          from **x** and **y** cannot arise, since such lines would cross.)

If no association line is present, the machine blocks.[13] If more than one
association line is present at the bottom (tonal) tier, the machine goes on as
before (given the above rule, it can only be an advance on the top tier) but
if the multiple association is at the top (syllable) tier, the machine blocks.
The reader can easily verify that this automaton, whose transition function
is tabulated below, will indeed accept all representations on which Tone
Mapping was correctly performed, and only these.

(6)

from **x** to **y**	from **x** to **z>y**	from **y** to **w>x**	automaton will
absent	any	any	block
present	present	any	block
present	absent	any	go on

2.3.3   Vowel projections

As our second example of explicating devices of phonological theory
in terms of automata, let us consider an automaton that is sensitive to
the content of the tiers. This automaton will accept all and only those

---

[13]It is convenient to permit failure on transition – alternatively, we could define a "sink
state" which is not an accepting state and every outgoing arc from it loops back to it.

representations which correspond to correct *vowel projections* (in the sense of section 1.3) such as (7A), and reject incorrect ones such as (7B) or (7C):

(7A)	(7B)	(7C)
barko	barko	barko
| |	| |	|
V V	V V	V

(8)

IS(x) is	y is	from x to y	from x to z>y	from y to w>x	automaton will
C	V	absent	any	any	go on
V	V	present	absent	absent	go on
X	V	present	absent	absent	go on

For the sake of simplicity the cases are not tabulated exhaustively. For instance if a symbol other than V appears on the bottom tier (and in all other cases not specifically listed above) the machine blocks. The reader can easily verify that the automaton defined this way will indeed accept only those bistrings where vowels (and segments underspecified for syllabicity) are associated to Vs one to one, and there are no other association lines.

2.3.4   A reduplicative template

As our third and final example of explicating phonological devices in terms of automata, let us consider the filling of the reduplicative CVC template that is used by Marantz 1982 to derive Agta reduplicated forms such as *taktakki* 'legs' or *ufuffu* 'thighs' from base forms *takki* 'leg' and *uffu* 'thigh'. Using the terminology introduced above, if the inherent skeleton of the stem begins with CVC, the whole reduplicative template is filled in, but if it begins with VC, the first C of the template remains unassociated. Following Clements 1985a I will assume that the association of Vs has priority, thus we have

(9A)   (9B)

    takki   uffu

     | |

    CVC   CVC

at an intermediate stage, after which both the t and the k of takki can associate, but the first C of the template in (9B) can no longer be associated, as that would result in crossing association lines.

in state	IS(x) is	y is	from x to y	from x to z>y	from y to w>x	automaton will
0	C	V	any	any	any	block
0	C	C	present	absent	absent	go to 1
0	V	V	any	any	any	block
0	V	C	present	any	any	block
0	V	C	absent	present	absent	go to 1
1	any	C	any	any	any	block
1	C	any	any	any	any	block
1	V	V	present	absent	absent	go to 2
2	C	C	present	absent	absent	go to 3
3	any	C	absent	absent	absent	go to 3

(Here again all configurations not explicitly listed are blocking the automaton.) With 3 as the only accepting state, the reader can easily verify that the automaton will accept representations such as (10A) and (10B), but not those in (10C) or (10D):

```
(10A)                    (10B)
    takki                    uffu
    | | |                    | |
    CVC                      CVC
```

```
(10C)                    (10D)
    takki                    uffu
    | | |/                   /| |
    CVC                      CVC
```

2.3.5   The role of automata

The most important weakness of the kind of formalization exemplified in
2.3.2-2.3.4 is that it is *inhomogeneous*. Rather than defining the overall
principles of association once and for all, one has to handcraft a separate automaton for each mapping principle, projection, or reduplicative
template. From a linguistic perspective, this makes the formalism too
powerful, because many other automata, not necessarily attested in actual
mapping principles, projections, or templatic patterns, are also definable
this way. Since from a mathematical perspective the formalism is very
weak (finite state mechanisms are at the bottom of the Chomsky hierarchy), this problem is not easy to remedy.

One possible approach is to bite the bullet and treat this formalism
the way one treats the formalism of calculus. Clearly it is an extremely
flexible and practical system and the fact that one can formulate within
it differential equations that do not correspond to any attested physical
phenomena does not detract from its usefulness in the description of
phenomena actually attested. The other approach, much more in keeping
with the tradition of phonological research, is to seek generalizations at a
higher level of abstraction. Rather than treating the automata themselves
as embodying linguistically significant generalizations, we look at the

way the automata are defined. For instance, the automaton defined in the last example above has the principle that Vs have priority in templatic association "hardwired" into its definition. But in fact the exact same automaton can be defined as the serial composition of two automata: one that checks the association of Vs and another that checks the association of Cs. Under such a decomposition, the linguistic principle of V-priority (Clements 1985a, Kiparsky 1987) is not part of the automata. Rather, it is encoded in the way the automata are put together (because the V-machine makes the first pass).

Now that we have evaluated the role that automata play in the formalization of autosegmental phonology, we are in a better position to answer the question raised at the beginning of this chapter: is autosegmental phonology only a notational gimmick? The answer is yes and no. To the extent that everything that can be done within an autosegmental framework can also be done with finite automata, the answer must be yes. But to the extent that the autosegmental notation gives rise to a new rule formalism, more capable of expressing linguistic generalizations in a notationally compact manner, the answer is no. The inhomogeneity discussed above is a general property of the automata (including the ones that perform linear encoding). Processes that receive a homogeneous formulation in autosegmental notation require a complex, often disjunctive, formulation if finite transducers are used. Since notational compactness is an important goal of linguistic theory, autosegmentalization is worth retaining.

2.4   Multi-tiered representations

The key technique of linear encoding used in the formalization of two-tiered representations (bistrings) does not generalize to the case of multi-tiered representations easily, because the basic rule governing the advancement of tapes can yield different results for different planes. Let us first illustrate this with an example:

(11)

```
d e f
|/  |
g h i
|/  |
j k l
```

As can be seen, the move after scanning (d,g,j) is ill-defined. On the top plane the presence of the line between d and g requires that we do not advance from g to h, while on the bottom plane the line between h and j requires advance from g to h. There are several ways out of this quandary – I will discuss the four major alternatives here.

2.4.1   Tuple notation

The top bistring in (11) can be encoded as $d1gte1gf0hbf1i$ and the bottom bistring can be encoded as $g1jth1ki0kbi1l$. Of these two we can form a 2-tuple

$$(d1gte1gf0hbf1i, g1jth1ki0kbi1l)$$

The advantage of this method is that it trivially generalizes to representations with more than three tiers. The chief disadvantage is that it is not iconic (in the sense of section 1.4) because changing a single element on the middle tier requires changes in both members of the tuple. A related problem is that the well-formedness of a representation, i.e. that the bottom tier of the top bistring is the same as the top tier of the bottom bistring, becomes extremely hard to check. These problems are better dealt with in the second approach discussed below.

2.4.2   Autosegmentalized tuples

The tuple $(d1gte1gf0hbf1i, g1jth1ki0kbi1l)$ of the previous approach can in fact be thought of as a bistring

(12)

```
d1gte1gf0hbf1i
  \ /  /   / \
  g1jth1ki0kbi1l
```

with the association lines drawn among the codes of the elements on the shared tier. This way, the problem of checking the well-formedness of the 2-tuple reduces to the problem of checking the appropriateness of the association lines in the corresponding bistring, a task that can easily be handled by autosegmental automata. Furthermore, the bistring can be encoded linearly. For the sake of better readability we add spaces, use T instead of t, B instead of b, 3 instead of 1, and 2 instead of 0 in the code strings themselves. This yields the code:

d0g t30g tg 1g tT0g te0g t30g tg 1g f0320jh 0Tbh 1h
B03f0k30i ti 1i bi 02bi 0kbi 0Bbi 1i bi 03bi 0l

This encoding, in spite of its forbidding look and considerable redundancy, is actually iconic in the sense that copies of the same token in the tristring (such as the nine copies of g and the ten copies of i) cannot appear arbitrarily far from one another. This guarantees that tristrings, much as bistrings, are also in the finite state domain.

While it is possible to generalize this scheme to multitiered representations with a larger number of tiers, the redundancy of the encoding grows exponentially in the number of tiers. For theoretical purposes, such as describing the generative power of phonological rules, this does not matter, but for practical purposes we need a better code.

2.4.3 Tier ordering

At the beginning of this section we saw that the simple rule of tape advancement given as (7) in chapter 1 leads to contradictions in multitiered representations. But if we replace this rule by a more complex rule, one that is designed for several tiers, a simpler encoding might still be possible. Many such replacements are conceivable. Here I will discuss only two, called *lazy advance* and *eager advance*.

In lazy advance, the tiers are linearly ordered. Tier 0 has the highest priority, tier 1 is next, and so on. The scanning head is advanced on tier 0 if this will not create a skipped association line. If it would, we try advancing the scanning head on tier 1, and so on. As long as the geometry of tiers (in the sense of Clements 1985b) is not circular, this approach will always work. This can be proved indirectly. Suppose that there is a multi-tiered representation with scanning heads on position t_0 on tier 0, t_1 on tier 1, and so on that is deadlocked. We cannot advance on tier 0, because there is an association line running from t_0 to some $m_i > t_i$ on tier i that would be skipped by this advance, $i > 0$. Similarly, we cannot advance on tier i, because there is an association line running from t_i to some $m_j > t_j$ on tier j that would be skipped by this advance, $j > i$. Since there are only finitely many tiers, sooner or later we must come to a tier k such that the head scanning t_k cannot be advanced, but there are no association lines running from t_k to any m_l such that $l > k, m_l > t_l$. But this is a contradiction, because the lazy rule says that in such a case we must advance t_k by one.

In eager advance, the tiers are unordered. We try to advance by one on as many of them as we can. Since (by similar reasoning as above) there can be no situation when no reading head can be advanced, at least one of them, and possibly all, will advance in any single move. Such a move is best depicted as an n-tuple of 0s (no movement) and 1s (advance), so for n tiers we have $2^n - 1$ possible moves. In the case of bistrings, (1,0) was denoted by t (top move), (0,1) was denoted by b (bottom move), and (1,1) was left unmarked. There are n letters, and $n - 1$ potential association lines under scan at any given moment. The machine can also notice further association lines going out of the positions under scan, otherwise it could not determine which tiers are to be advanced next. The presence or absence of association lines, the letters under scan, and the internal state of the finite state control will determine its subsequent internal state and position of scanning heads. Given the possibility of the kind of linear encoding described in 2.4.2, such multi-tier automata do not create an increase in generative power as compared to the (two-tier) autosegmental automata discussed so far (and defined more rigorously in the Appendix).

2.4.4   A distinguished timing tier

The discussion of multi-tiered representations would not be complete without mentioning the one method that is actually used for linearization in phonological theory, namely the use of a distinguished *timing tier*. While a formal treatment has to be deferred until chapter 4, the basic idea can be informally stated here as follows.

One distinguished tier is used for encoding timing information. Roughly speaking, one cell on the tape corresponding to this tier is approximately 80 ms. long, i.e. corresponds to the average duration of a short segment. The exact duration of the segment will then be determined by rules of phonetic interpretation sensitive to stress, segmental context, etc., much as in Klatt's model of segmental duration discussed in section 3.1 below[14]. In the original version of the theory (Clements and Keyser 1983) the timing tier also contains information about the syllabicity of segments, but in the more widely accepted contemporary version (Levin 1985) it is devoted entirely to the encoding of coarse-grained timing information.

All other tiers receive temporal interpretation through the distinguished timing tier. Feature F precedes, follows, or overlaps feature H if the timing units associated to F precede, follow, or overlap those of H. In terms of the multi-tiered automata introduced in 2.4.3 above, this conception is closer to lazy than to eager advance – tier 0 (the one with the highest priority) is the timing tier and advancement along this

---

[14]The chief difference from Klatt's model is that here every segment starts with the same INHDUR, except for long ones (geminates) which have two timing units.

tier is what corresponds to the flow of time. But there is an important difference. While in lazy advancement it is the association pattern that dictates the next move, so that several moves might be required to make actual advance on tier 0, in the timing tier conception all such moves are performed within a single timing unit.

Therefore, the timing tier concept involves a kind of time warping. The time periods between successive moves of the automaton are not constant, except in the special case when a single move accomplishes an advancement on the timing tier. But if it takes n moves to get to the new cell on the timing tier, each move is assumed to have taken only $1/n$ units of time. The situation is further complicated by the fact that most tiers link to the timing tier only indirectly, via *class node* tiers (see Clements 1985b) and by the fact that the association of two nodes means only that they are overlapping, *not* that they are coterminous (Sagey 1988, Bird and Klein 1990). After developing a phonetically more realistic model of duration in chapter 3, we will return to this issue in chapter 4.

2.5 Appendix

In section 2.3 we informally defined biautomata and gave some examples. Here we will concentrate on a seemingly more complex, but in fact less powerful (and more coherent) class of autosegmental automata that will be called, for reasons that will become apparent, *regular*. Since all the linguistic burden carried by biautomata can be carried by the mathematically more coherent class of regular autosegmental automata, the distinction between the two is important only to readers interested in the finer details of autosegmental generative capacity – others can simply skip ahead to 2.5.3. In 2.5.1 some simple examples of bilanguages are analyzed, and two finitistic classes of autosegmental automata are defined: *nondeterministically advancing* and *regular*. The key result about regular automata, Kleene's theorem, is proved in 2.5.2, where the relationship between various classes of automata, regular expressions, and (non)determinism are investigated. The results are then applied in 2.5.3 to a deeper analysis of reduplication and the OCP.

2.5.1   Finite-stateness and regularity

Let us begin by defining a **nondeterministically advancing autosegmental automaton** (or na^2-automaton for short) as a 6-tuple (S, T, U, i, F, t) where S is a set of states, T and U are the alphabets of the two tapes, i is the initial state, F is the set of final (accepting) states, and t is the transition function. As before, if we denote the cell under scan on the upper tape by **x**, the cell under scan on the lower tape by **y**, the transition function from a given state depends on the following factors:

(i) Is there a symbol[15] in cell **x**, and, if so, what symbol?

(ii) Is there a symbol in cell **y**, and, if so, what symbol?

(iii) Is there an association line between the symbol in **x** and the symbol in **y**?

(iv) Are there further association lines from **x** to some symbol after **y**?

(v) Are there further association lines from **y** to some symbol after **x**?

The transition function t, depending on the present state, the letters under scan, and the presence of association lines to these letters, will assign a new state, and advance the tapes in accordance with the following rule (compare rule (7) in chapter 1):

> If there are no further association lines from **x** and **y**, both tapes can move one step to the right, if there are further association lines from **x**, only the bottom tape can move, and if there are further association lines from **y**, only the top tape can move.

---

[15]The case where there is no symbol under scan is represented by the special symbol G introduced in section 1.3.

To specify which tape *does* move, it is best to separate out the transition function into three separate components: one that gives the new state, provided a top move t was taken; one that gives the new state, provided a bottom move b was taken; and one that gives the new state, provided a full move f was taken. Here and in what follows $x[y, t]$ denotes the result state of making a top move from state x upon input y, and similarly for $x[y, b]$ (bottom move) and $x[y, f]$ (full move). In a nondeterministic version there can be more than one such state, and we do not require that only a top, bottom, or full move be available at any given point[16].

Such automata are capable of accepting non-finite-state bilanguages or, if used as coders, can generate arbitrarily large code strings from fixed, limited length autosegmental representations. In chapter 1.4, where our interest was in coding, we removed the nondeterminism from the scanning process and thus guaranteed a unique code. But the underlying cause of non-finite-stateness is not the lack of determinism in the transition function. As we shall see shortly, deterministically advancing biautomata can still accept non-finite-state bilanguages.

Before giving an example, we first have to provide an automaton-free characterization of what we mean by *finite-state* or *regular*. This is done by carrying over a definition from the linear case. Define the **syntactic congruence** $\equiv_L$ generated by a bilanguage L as containing those pairs of bistrings (α, β) which are freely substitutable for one another, i.e. for which $\gamma\alpha\delta \in L \Leftrightarrow \gamma\beta\delta \in L$. When γ (δ) is fixed as the empty string, we will talk of right (left) congruence. As in the linear case, we define a bilanguage to be **regular** iff it gives rise to a (right)congruence with finitely many classes, and as in the linear case, we shall show that there is an equivalent characterization by suitable finite automata (but *not* by biautomata).

Let us denote the bistring composed of i floating features on the top tier and j floating features on the bottom tier by $< i, j >$, and consider

---

[16] It might still be the case that only one of these moves is available, because that is what the association pattern dictates, but there is no general requirement enforcing uniqueness of next move.

the bilanguage $B = \{< i,i > | i > 0\}$. Is it regular? At first sight, it appears to be, both because its linear encoding $C(B)$ is the regular language 0^+, and because it can be expressed as the Kleene-closure $^+$ of the one-member bilanguage $\{< 1,1 >\}$. But by the above definition it is not regular, since the bistrings $< 1,k >$ all belong in different (right)congruence classes for $k = 1,2,...$ as can be seen using $\delta = < l,1 >$. If $k \neq l$ then $< 1,k >< l,1 > \notin B$ but $< 1,l >< l,1 > \in B$.

While this result is initially a little surprising (and will require a more careful approach to what we mean by "regular expression" in the autosegmental case), the more we look at it the less desirable it appears to call B 'regular'. However we define 'regular' for bilanguages, it is a good idea to retain as many of the properties of regular stringsets as possible. For instance, regular stringsets are closed under regular transduction (generalized sequential mapping), and the mapping that introduces association lines optionally is certainly sequential. From B this mapping produces the bilanguage A of well-formed bistrings with an equal number of features on the two tiers – so if B was regular, A should be regular too. But this is quite unnatural, given that its code $C(A)$ is properly context-free.

By careful analysis of where context-freeness creeps in, we can pinpoint the source of the difficulty. The reason why $C(A)$ is not regular is that it contains every string that has an equal number of ts and bs. $C(B)$ is a special case, strings in it contain an equal number, namely 0, ts and bs. But in a sense there are ts and bs hidden in the deterministic advancement on both tiers, where the tb (or equivalently bt) move is left unencoded. If the bilanguage B was encoded by the kind of biautomaton defined above, it would then be the case that we get each code string that has an equal number of ts and bs. Why is this so bad? After all, a full move f should be equivalent to a tb and to a bt move sequence, and such sequences will of necessity give rise to an equal number of ts and bs.

The problem manifests itself on end condition, when the machine is about to fall off of one or both of the tiers. In such cases, automatic advancement does not treat tb and bt equally. For example if we start the machine at the beginning of $< 1, 2 >$, a tb sequence would fail with the bottom head scanning the first feature, while a bt sequence would fail with the bottom head scanning the second feature. This suggests the following definition: the transition function at state u $\in$ S is **scanning independent** iff every possible scanning of a string α takes the machine from u to the same state x=u[α]. In particular, a full move should be equivalent to a sequence of a top move followed by a bottom move, as well as to a bottom move followed by a top move, two full moves should be replaceable by $ttbb$, $bbtt$, $tbtb$, $bttb$, $tbbt$, $btbt$ and similarly for fff and longer sequences of moves. A na²-automaton will be called a **regular autosegmental automaton** iff its transition function is scanning independent at every state. As we shall see in 2.5.2 below, the use of the term 'regular' is justified by the validity of Kleene's theorem.

2.5.2   The characterization of regular bilanguages

At this point, we have two independent notions of regular bilanguages, one defined by the finite index property of the syntactic congruence, and one by acceptance by a regular autosegmental automaton. Our goal here is to extend Kleene's theorem to the autosegmental domain by showing that these two notions are equivalent with one another, and with several other characterizations via regular expressions, closure under operations, and code sets.

First note that nondeterministic regular autosegmental automata can always be replaced by deterministic ones. The proof is exactly the same as for the standard (linear) case. Instead of the state set S of the nondeterministic automaton, consider its power set 2^S and "lift" the non-deterministic transition function t to a deterministic transition function d the following way. For $i \in$ S define d($\{i\}$) as $\{t(i)\}$, and for $X \subset$ S, $d(X) = \bigcup_{i \in X} d(\{i\})$. The proof will not generalize to the coder case, because different nondeterministic options can lead to different positioning of the heads. However, if the transition function is scanning independent, different positionings of the heads can always be exchanged without altering the eventual state of the machine.

Thus we have three families of bilanguages. Those accepted by finite autosegmental automata (deterministic or nondeterministic) will be collected in the family **R**, those accepted by na^2-automata will be collected in the family **NA**, and those accepted by biautomata will be collected in the family **B**. Clearly we have **R** $\subset$ **NA, B** $\subset$ **NA**, since both scanning independence and deterministic advancing are additional properties to those required in the general class of biautomata. As we shall see below, where the "geography" of these classes is investigated, both of these inclusions are proper. Let us prove Kleene's theorem first.

Theorem 1. A bilanguage L is in **R** iff the right congruence $\equiv_L$ generated by it has finitely many classes.

Proof. If L is accepted by a regular autosegmental automaton, it is also accepted by a deterministic regular autosegmental automaton (which can be constructed by the method outlined above) and further it can be accepted by a reduced automaton in which no two states have exactly the same transition function (for such states can always be collapsed into a single state). We claim that there will be as many right congruence classes in $\equiv_L$ as there are states in a minimal (reduced, deterministic, regular) autosegmental automaton $A=(S, T, U, i, F, t)$.

To see this, define $\alpha \equiv_A \beta$ iff for every scanning of α starting in the initial state i and ending in some state j there is a scanning of β starting in i and also ending in j and vice versa. Clearly, $\equiv_A$ is an equivalence relation, and $\alpha \equiv_A \beta \Rightarrow \alpha \equiv_L \beta$. If $\alpha \not\equiv_A \beta$, there must exist a state j such that at least one scanning of one of the bistrings, say α, will lead from i to j, but no scanning of β will ever lead from i to j. Since A is deterministic, scanning β will lead to some state k$\neq$j. We will show that there exists a string δ such that from j we get to an accepting state by scanning δ and from k we get to a non-accepting state (or conversely), meaning that $\alpha\delta \in L$ but $\beta\delta \notin L$ (or conversely), so in either case $\alpha \not\equiv_L \beta$.

Call two states p and q *distinguishable* iff there exists a string δ such that starting from p, scanning δ leads to an accepting state, but starting from q, scanning δ leads to a rejecting state or vice versa. *In*distinguishability, denoted by I, is an equivalence relation. Clearly, pIp holds for every state p, and if pIq, also qIp. For transitivity, suppose indirectly that pIq and qIr, but p and r are distinguishable, i.e. there is a string δ for which p[δ] is accepting but r[δ] is not. Now, q[δ] is either accepting or rejecting. In the former case, qIr was false, and in the latter, pIq was false, contradiction. Further, in a minimal automaton there can be no two (or more) indistinguishable states, for such states could be collapsed into a single state without altering the accepted bilanguage. Since j and k above are not equal, they are distinguishable by some δ, which proves the "if" part.

To prove the "only if" part of the theorem, we have to show that if a bilanguage L gives rise to a finite right congruence, it is accepted by some regular autosegmental automaton. We will construct the states of the automaton from the congruence classes of the equivalence relation. Let us denote the congruence class of a bistring α under $\equiv_L$ by (α). The initial state of the machine is the congruence class of the empty bistring, ( ), and the transition function from state (α) is defined the following way.

Recall that t-catenation of a feature T (on the top tier) to some bistring α was defined in chapter 1 as associating T with the last feature on the bottom tier of α, and analogously b-catenation of a feature B (on the bottom tier) to some bistring α is defined by associating B with the last feature on the top tier of α. The result will be denoted by αtT and αbB respectively. (Ordinary concatenation of bistrings α and β will be denoted by $\alpha\beta$ as before.) Now, the result state of a top transition from (α) can be defined as the congruence class (αtT) and similarly the result state of a bottom transition from (α) will be the congruence class (αbB). Thus top (bottom) transitions are nondeterministic – there are as many result states as there are congruence classes for each member of the top (bottom) tier alphabet. For ordinary concatenation of a bistring β, the result is defined by the class $(\alpha\beta)$, so as to guarantee scanning independence.

Finally, the accepting states of the automaton are defined as those congruence classes that contain the members of L – this is well-defined because if $\alpha \equiv_L \beta$, both must be members of L or both must be outside L (meaning that L is a union of congruence classes). What remains to be seen is that the bilanguage M accepted by the automaton defined here is the same as the bilanguage L we started with. First let us take a bistring α included in L – since (α) is an accepting state, it follows that α is also in M. Next let us take a bistring β not in L – since (β) is not an accepting state it would follow that β is not in M if we can show that no scanning path would lead to any state other than (β). This can be done by induction on the length (defined as the maximum of the length of the top and bottom strings) of β. For length one, i.e. when C(β)=x0y or x1y, $\beta \notin L$ is trivial, since the scanning path is unique.

If it is true for all βs of length $k < n$, it will also be true of βs of length n, but the proof is complicated by the fact that such bistrings can arise in several ways (as discussed under (12) in chapter 1.6). When the code of β contains two adjacent numbers, i.e. when there was a full move during scan, the parts preceding and following the break where the full move occurs are guaranteed to be shorter than n, so the induction step is complete. But when there was no break, i.e. when all moves during scan were top or bottom moves, splitting up the bistring would be a more complex matter. Fortunately, in such cases the scanning is uniquely determined by the association pattern, so the induction completing the proof of Theorem 1. can be trivially performed on the number of moves instead.

Now that **R** is established as a coherent class we can investigate its relationship to **B** and **NA** more fully. Let us consider the bilanguage $T = \{<i,j> 1|i > j\}$ – it contains those bistrings that have i floating features on the top tier, j floating features on the bottom tier, followed by an end marker '1' which is simply a feature on the top tier associated to a feature on the bottom tier. Clearly, if $i - j \neq i' - j'$, then $< i, j > \neq_T$ $< i', j' >$, so T is not in **R**. However, it is in **B**, since the following automaton will accept it:

(13)

in state	from x to y	from x to z>y	from y to w>x	automaton will
0	absent	absent	absent	stay in 0
0	absent	absent	present	go to 1
1	absent	absent	present	stay in 1
1	present	absent	absent	go to 2
2	any	any	any	go to 3

With 2 as the only accepting state, the machine will accept only those strings whose scan puts the machine in 2, but not further. To get into 2, the last thing the machine must encounter is a single association line (the end marker) in state 1. To get into state 1, the machine can make a number of top moves over floating elements (this is the loop over state 1) preceded by a number of full moves over floating elements (this is the loop over state 0). Note that this is not scanning independent – no provision was made for top and bottom moves to replace full moves out of state 0.

What this example shows is that **B** is not contained in **R**. It is, of course, contained in **NA**, and the bilanguage B introduced above shows that the containment is proper. The biautomaton that accepts this bilanguage is trivial – it contains only one state and only full advance is permitted (and that only when no association lines are present). To see that no biautomaton can accept this bilanguage, suppose indirectly that an n-state biautomaton A accepts B. The bistrings $(x0y)^k$ are all accepted

$(k = 1, 2, 3, ..., n + 1)$, so there is at least one accepting state f which accepts both $(x0y)^i$ and $(x0y)^j$, $1 \leq i < j \leq n + 1$, by the pigeonhole principle. Let $j - i = p$, and consider the bistring $< j, i >$. In the first i steps, we arrive in f, and in the next p steps we make legal top moves (since we are at the end of the bottom string) which are indistinguishable from legal full moves. But p full moves would take as back to f, which is an accepting state, so p top moves also take us back to f, meaning that $< j, i >$ is accepted by A, contradiction. To complete our "geographic survey", note that **R** is not contained in **B**. This can be seen e.g. by considering the regular bilanguage $D = \{< 1, j > | j > 0\}$. Collecting these results gives us

Theorem 2. Both **R** and **B** are properly contained in **NA**, but neither is contained in the other.

Let us consider how **R** can be characterized by operations. It is closed under union and intersection as the standard direct product construction shows, and also under complementation (as can be trivially established both from the finite index property and from the characterization by automata) – the group of boolean operations offers no surprises. But the group of string operations, namely concatenation and Kleene-closure, requires considerable revision if we move to the domain of bistrings. If we use concatenation as the only "succession" operation, we have a problem in that there are an infinite number of further undecomposable structures, such as the bistrings encoded as $1(t1)^*$ (or $1(b1)^*$), which correspond to the spreading of a single element on the bottom (top) tier. These structures, and many others, have no structural break in them if indeed concatenation was the only possibility. That is why we introduced t-catenation and b-catenation above.

    Once these operations are available for creating larger bistrings from two successive bistrings, **Kleene-closure** will include these as well. This way the "mystery" of bilanguage B introduced in 2.5.1 above disappears. $B = \{< i, i > | i > 0\}$ is *not* the Kleene $^+$ of $< 1, 1 >$, because the closure means arbitrarily many catenation operations *includ-ing* t-catenations and b-catenations. The Kleene $^+$ of $< 1, 1 >$ is really $\{< i, j > | i, j > 0\}$, which is of course regular. From the characterization by automata it easily follows that the concatenation, t-catenation, b-catenation, and Kleene-closure of regular bilanguages is again regular. Standard proofs will also generalize for closure under (inverse) homomorphisms and (inverse) transductions. Since closure under transduction is particularly relevant for the method of replacing phonological rules by transducers, let us state this in a separate

Theorem 3. If L is a regular bilanguage and G = (S, I, O, i, F, T), a generalized bisequential mapping, the image (L)G of L under G is also regular.

Proof. First we create a trace of the GSM transducing a bistring α over some top tier alphabet P and bottom tier alphabet Q. In a single step, G scans some letter p on the top tier, q on the bottom tier. Depending on these, on the presence of association lines (see 2.5.1), and on its current state s_i, G will scanning independently advance the tapes, move to some state s_j, and add a bistring α (by concatenation, t-catenation, or b-catenation) to the output created so far. Since there are only finitely many bistrings in T, we can create a finite alphabet of 10-tuples (s_i, p, q, b_1, b_2, b_3, n_1, n_2, α , s_j) corresponding to such elementary moves. s_i is the state of G before transition, p (q) is the symbol under scan on the top (bottom) tier before transition, b_1 is 1 or 0 depending on whether an association line between x and y was present, b_2 (b_3) is 1 or 0 depending on whether an association line from x (y) to some further element on the bottom (top) tier was present, n_1 is $t\,b$ or f depending on the move taken on the input string, n_2 is $t\,b$ or f depending on the catenation operation used for output, α is the output, and s_j is the resulting state.

The idea of the proof (modeled after Salomaa 1973, Ch. 4) is to encode the generalized sequential mapping in strings of 10-tuples. Those that correspond to the action of the GSM on some input bistring will homomorphically yield sequences of 4-tuples (p,b_1,q,n_1) that give linear encodings of the input string, and similarly the concatenation of 2-tuples (α, n_2) gives a linear encoding of the output string. Thus if we show that any regular bilanguage is the inverse homomorphic image of a regular language of 4-tuple codes, and filter out those 10-tuple sequences that do not correspond to well-formed transductions (e.g. because the first member of the first 10-tuple is not the initial state of the GSM), the 2-tuple code of the output bilanguage can be obtained from the resulting stringset by homomorphism. Since the filtering involves the intersection of a regular language with regular sets, what remains to be seen is that the encoding of a regular bilanguage is a regular language and, conversely, the decoding of a regular language is a regular bilanguage, which is trivial for the scanning invariant encodings/decoding.[17]

We have seen that the family **R** of bilanguages is closed under the boolean operations, catenation operations, and mappings and thus appears as a perfect analog of the regular family of string languages. The final step in characterizing regular bilanguages is to show that a "regular expression" characterization is also available for regular bilanguages. It is a good exercise to prove the following

Theorem 4. Every bilanguage accepted by an autosegmental automaton can be built up from elementary ones by union, t-catenation, b-catenation, concatenation, and Kleene-closure.

2.5.3 Implications for phonology

Now that the foundations of formal bilanguage theory have been laid, it is perhaps time to stop for a minute and take stock. What have the first two chapters accomplished? At the conceptual level, the basic ideas of autosegmental phonology have been explicated in a relatively simple but

---

[17]As the example of the language B shows, scanning invariance is crucial here – the linear code introduced in chapter 1.4 can yield regular stringsets from non-regular bilanguages.

rigorous theory analogous to that of formal languages. At the practical level, the method of linear encoding enables us to do autosegmental phonology using the algorithms already in place for linear phonology. But the formal method offers more than an answer to *what* things are and *how* they work, it offers insight into *why* things are the way they are. Here I will consider two rather puzzling aspects of autosegmental phonology: the proliferation of theories of reduplication, and the OCP.

After the spectacular success of autosegmental phonology in eliminating root-and-pattern infixation from the inventory of rules (McCarthy 1979), most phonologists subscribed to the broader program of eliminating transformational rules altogether. One of the prime targets of the effort to streamline the rule component was, and continues to be, reduplication. Starting with Marantz 1982 a new autosegmental account of reduplication appears almost every year. Why do we see this proliferation of theories? The obvious answer would be that they are empirically inadequate (as argued e.g. in Carrier-Duncan 1984). But many empirically inadequate theories remain unchallenged for years, and we can safely conclude that the real reason lies deeper. The problem is not that these theories cannot account for the data, for that can always be fixed, but rather the fact that they fail to carry out the promised reduction. As we noted in 2.2.4 above *all* theories of reduplication make essential use of some otherwise unmotivated operation.

Can one day a more clever phonologist come along and eliminate reduplication without introducing some other operation or abandoning some fundamental tenet of autosegmental phonology at the same time? The formal theory developed here enables us to answer this question in the negative. It has been widely recognized that the power of the reduplication transformation is not within the reach of autosegmental phonology. xx languages, such as created by full stem or word reduplication, were known from the outset to be outside the regular domain. What has not been recognized is that limited length, templatic reduplication is also outside the domain of autosegmental phonology as long as it is viewed as a structured class of problems (in the sense of 2.2.4).

Two identical copies of any string, appearing on two tiers, and associated feature by feature, are easy to create by finitistic methods (using biautomata). This is the *copy* or *transfer* stage of the derivation. It is also possible to dissociate the two strings by finitistic methods – what is not possible is to linearize the results. Using the techniques developed so far it is easy to show that the language Z of matching strings with a single association line running from the last feature on the top tier to the first feature on the bottom tier is outside **NA**, and thus outside **B** and **R**. But if we had a general-purpose algorithm of the kind theories of reduplication attempt to create, i.e. one that would work for any arbitrary CV template, xx languages were possible to generate by regular autosegmental rules, so Z would also be possible, contradiction.

Not only does this analysis pinpoint the reason for the failure of existing theories of reduplication – it also explains their partial success. Clearly, as long as instances of reduplication rules in various languages are viewed as an unstructured collection of problems, it is possible to devise a solution to any such collection as long as it does not contain unbounded cases. In other words, it is not the individual cases, but precisely the attempt to integrate these into a structured, perhaps even parameterized, "theory of reduplication" that leads, of necessity, to the introduction of some extraordinary device.

The **Obligatory Contour Principle** (OCP) of Leben 1973 has been an important part of autosegmental phonology since the initial development of the theory. In its basic form, the principle states that contours (sequences of non-identical features) are obligatory, i.e. that sequences of identical features are disallowed, at least in underlying representations. Without attempting to do justice to the complex discussion surrounding it (see e.g. Odden 1986, Hayes 1986, Schein and Steriade 1986, Yip 1988, Odden 1988), here I will focus on one rather puzzling aspect of the OCP, namely that all kinds of dissimilatory lexical constraints are explained on the basis of it (see e.g. McCarthy 1988). What makes such a simple principle able to carry so heavy an explanatory burden?

The answer is to be found in the relationship of contours and advancement along the tiers. The finite state control of autosegmental automata can move to a new state on the basis of detecting a different feature or a new association pattern. But if the features on one tier become identical in value and association pattern, the automaton must repeat a cycle of states. In the simplest possible case, this cycle will be a loop over a single state, in the next simplest case the cycle will involve alternation between two states, and so on. Conceptually, the OCP corresponds to the simplest case. In automatic advancement a machine remaining in the same state cannot distinguish between the bistrings $< i, 1 >$ for arbitrarily large i, i.e. a sequence of identical features will be indistinguishable from a single feature.

Thus the OCP appears not as an inviolable pattern but as the simplest case within a hierarchy of increasingly complex patterns. The next case, alternation between two states, is widely attested in the construction of metrical feet from syllables. The case after that, ternary feet construction, is only sporadically attested, if at all, and there are no known examples of quaternary cycles. The OCP can exert such a wide influence because it is the simplest possible case. In terms of autosegmental automata the kind encountered most often in phonology is the looping kind (where accepting states are final), and such automata will necessarily show OCP effects.

The conclusion I would like to draw from these examples of looking at autosegmental phonology from a finite state perspective is that the formalism developed here is loose only superficially, to the extent that it makes possible to state phonological rules which are nowhere attested. But in a more fundamental respect the regularity of the formalism gives us a rather tight grip on phonology, because it imposes a powerful constraint on the languages characterizable by autosegmental means.

2.5.4 Subsequent work

Wiebe (1992) realized that the tuple notation proposed in 2.4.1 above for 3-strings and in general for k-strings with $k \geq 3$ will be applicable for $k = 2$ (bistrings) if we simply flag each element on each tier with the number of association lines it has (expressing the number in base one). For example, for the bistrings listed in (1:15) and repeated here for convenience,

(14)

```
a k c d e f g h
| / /   /   | /
H H L M H L M
```

Wiebe would have a 2-tuple *(a1k1c1de1f1g1h, H11H1LM1HL11M)*. As he notes, this coding scheme is far easier to extend to $k \geq 3$ than the linear codes proposed in chapter 1.4 above because the 2-tuples extend naturally to k-tuples and the identity of the association lines can be maintained by using a separate unary base symbol for each plane. For example, if we use the symbol '1' for the plane between the top and the middle tier and '2' for the plane between the middle and the bottom tier in the representation given in (11) above and repeated here for convenience,

(15)

```
d e f
| /  |
g h i
| /  |
j k l
```

Wiebe's tuple encoding would yield *(d1e1f1,g112h2i12,j22kl2)*. Another advantage of this code is that it easily extends to degenerate cases where one or more of the tiers is empty or where the graph encoding the tiers permitted to have associated nodes (called the *geometry* of features, see section 4.1) is not required to be a tree. Also, ordinary multi-tape finite automata are now applicable since the association lines going to cells on the i-th tier are now encoded in the i-th member of the tuple. However, the larger program of reducing the autosegmental case $(k > 1)$ to the study of the linear case $(k = 1)$ is no longer feasible in this framework.

A similar k-tuple encoding is presented in Bird and Ellison 1994 as part of a larger program of compiling autosegmental representations into regular expressions and finite automata. Unlike Wiebe 1992, Bird and Ellison accept the conclusion of chapter 2.2 that autosegmental phonology is regular, and provide a method for directly expressing phonological constraints as finite automata. The major differences between the formalization presented here and that of Bird and Ellison are the *monotonicity* and the *soft semantics* of their system. Monotonicity will be discussed in greater detail in chapter 4 – here it is sufficient to say that Bird and Ellison use constraints in a genuinely monotonic, monostratal setting, while the present work uses a multistratal setting which does not exclude non-monotonic analyses.

The present work has *strict semantics* in the sense that the notion **subrepresentation of** requires the association lines to be explicitly listed. For example the structure given by $(c, y, \{(2, 1)\})$ is a sub-APR of (16) but $(b, x, \{(1, 0)\})$ is not.

(16)

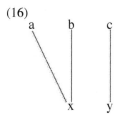

The semantics is strict inasmuch as a rule with SD $(b, x, \{(1, 0)\})$ would not be triggered in this environment.[18] In other words, ordinary concatenation (as opposed to t-catenation or b-catenation) plays a distinguished

---

[18]This is exactly as required by the Linking Constraint of Hayes 1986.

role in decomposing the input to a locus and a context of rule application. But for Bird and Ellison, rule application means constraint superposition, and *subrepresentation of* is defined simply by the *subset of* relationship.

One particularly noteworthy consequence of this approach is that sequences of two identical segments become semantically indistinguishable from geminates. A sequence of two short vowels *aa* as in (17A) and a long vowel *a:* as in (17B) will, by the Bird and Ellison algorithm, be encoded in the 2-tuples $(V : 1 + V : 1) \sqcap (a : 1 + a : 1)$ and $(V : 1 + V : 1) \sqcap (a : 2)$ respectively.

(17A)   (17B)

As we convert these 2-tuples to regular expressions, the first will yield $(V \cap a)^+ (V \cap a)^* (V \cap a)^+$ while the second will yield $(V \cap a)^+ (V \cap a)^+$. Though syntactically different, semantically these terms are equivalent, since the * term can be absorbed in the $^+$ terms. Because a large number of phonological rules, both lexical and postlexical, are sensitive to the difference between a sequence of two identical short segments and a single long segment, the semantics of (17A) and (17B) must be kept distinct. In earlier versions of the formalism such as Bird and Klein 1989 this could be accomplished by inserting a phonetically unrealized *point event* between the two segments in (17A), but in the current version the use of such devices cannot be reconciled with the overall claim to monotonicity.

2.6 References

Anderson, Stephen R. 1992. *A-Morphous Morphology*. Cambridge University Press.

Archangeli, Diana 1985. Yokuts harmony: evidence for coplanar representation in nonlinear phonology. *Linguistic Inquiry* **16** 335–372.

Aronoff, Mark 1976. *Word formation in generative grammar*. MIT Press, Cambridge.

Bagemihl, Bruce 1989. The crossing constraint and 'Backwards Languages'. *Natural Language and Linguistic Theory* **7** 481–549.

Baker, James K. 1979. Trainable grammars for speech recognition. In *Speech Communication Papers for the 97th Meeting of the ASA*, D.H. Klatt and J.J. Wolf, (eds.) 547–550.

Bird, Steven and T. Mark Ellison 1994. One-level phonology: autosegmental representations and rules as finite automata. *Computational Linguistics* **20** 1 .

Bird, Steven and Ewan Klein 1989. Phonological Events, University of Edinburgh Centre for Cognitive Science, EUCCS/RP-24.

Bird, Steven and Ewan H. Klein 1990. Phonological events. *Journal of Linguistics* **26** 33–56.

Cannon, Robert L. 1975. Phrase Structure Grammars Generating Context-Free Languages. *Information and Control* **29** 252–267.

Carden, Guy 1983. The non-finite=state-ness of the word formation component. *Linguistic Inquiry* **14** 537–541.

Carrier-Duncan, J. 1984. Some problems with prosodic accounts of reduplication. In *Language Sound Structure*, Mark Aronoff and Richard T. Oehrle, (eds.) MIT Press, 260–286.

Chomsky, Noam 1957. *Syntactic Structures*. Mouton, The Hague.

Chomsky, Noam 1959. On certain formal properties of grammars. *Information and Control* **2** 137–167.

Chomsky, Noam 1962.   Context-free grammars and pushdown storage. *MIT Electronics Research Lab Quarterly Progress Report* **65**.

Chomsky, Noam 1965.   *Aspects of the theory of syntax.* MIT Press, Cambridge MA.

Chomsky, Noam and Morris Halle 1968.   *The Sound Pattern of English.* Harper & Row, New York.

Clements, George N. 1985a.   The problem of transfer in nonlinear phonology. *Cornell Working Papers in Linguistics* **5** 38–73.

Clements, George N. 1985.   The geometry of phonological features. *Phonology Yearbook* **2** 225–252.

Clements, George N. and Kevin C. Ford 1979.   Kikuyu Tone Shift and its Synchronic Consequences. *Linguistic Inquiry* **10** 179–210.

Clements, George N. and S. Jay Keyser 1983.   *CV Phonology: A Generative Theory of the Syllable.* MIT Press, Cambridge.

Cole, Jennifer S. 1987.   *Planar phonology and morphology.* PhD Thesis, MIT.

Culy, Christopher 1985.   The complexity of the vocabulary of Bambara. *Linguistics and Philosophy* **8** 345–351.

Dressler, Wolfgang U. 1985.   *Morphonology: the dynamics of derivation.* Karoma, Ann Arbor.

Farkas, Donka and Patrice Beddor 1987.   Privative and Equipollent Backness in Hungarian. In *Parasession on Autosegmental and Metrical Phonology, CLS 23.*

Flanagan, J. 1972.   *Speech Analysis, Synthesis and Perception.* Springer Verlag, New York.

Halle, Morris and Jean-Roger Vergnaud 1987.   *An essay on stress.* MIT Press, Cambridge.

Hayes, Bruce 1984.   The phonology of rhythm in English. *Linguistic Inquiry* **15** 33–74.

Hayes, Bruce 1986.   Inalterability in CV phonology. *Language* **62** 321–351.

Hulst, Harry van der   1988.   The geometry of vocalic features, Leiden Papers in Linguistics and Phonetics.

Itô, Junko 1989.   A prosodic theory of epenthesis. *Natural Language and Linguistic Theory* **7** 217–260.

Johnson, Ch. Douglas 1970.   *Formal aspects of phonological representation*. PhD Thesis, UC Berkeley.

Kager, Reneé and Ellis Visch 1988.   Metrical constituency and rhythmic adjustment. *Phonology* **5** 21–72.

Kahn, Daniel 1976.   *Syllable-based Generalizations in English Phonology*. PhD Thesis, MIT.

Kaplan, Ronald and Martin Kay ms.   *Phonological rules and finite state transducers*. Xerox PARC.

Kenstowicz, Michael and Charles Kisseberth 1973.   The multiple application problem in phonology. In *Studies in generative phonology*, Charles Kisseberth, (ed.) Linguistic Research Inc., Edmonton, 1–12.

Kiparsky, Paul 1982.   Lexical morphology and phonology. In *Linguistics in the morning calm*, I.-S. Yang, (ed.) Hanshin, Seoul, 3–91.

Kiparsky, Paul   1987.   The Phonology of Reduplication, Ms, Stanford University.

Knuth, Donald E. 1968.   Semantics of context-free languages. *Mathematical Systems Theory* **2** 127–145.

Kornai, András 1994.   *On Hungarian morphology*. Hungarian Academy of Sciences Institute of Linguistics, Budapest.

Koutsoudas, Andreas 1976.   Unordered rule hypotheses. In *The Application and Ordering of Grammatical Rules*, Andreas Koutsoudas, (ed.) Mouton, The Hague, 1–21.

Leben, William 1973.   *Suprasegmental phonology*. PhD Thesis, MIT.

Levin, Juliette 1985. *A metrical theory of syllabicity*. PhD Thesis, MIT.

Lieber, Rochelle 1981. Morphological conversion within a restrictive theory of the lexicon. In *Linguistic Models*, M. Moortgat, H. van der Hulst and T. Hoekstra, (eds.) Foris, Dordrecht, 161–200.

Marantz, Alec 1982. Re Reduplication. *Linguistic Inquiry* **13** 435–482.

Matthews, G.H. 1963. Discontinuity and Asymmetry in Phrase Structure Grammars. *Information and Control* **6** 137–146.

Maurer, H.A., A. Salomaa and D. Wood 1980. Pure grammars. *Information and Control* **44** 47–72.

McCarthy, John J. 1979. *Formal Problems in Semitic Phonology and Morphology*. PhD Thesis, MIT.

McCarthy, John J. 1981. A prosodic theory of nonconcatenative morphology. *Linguistic Inquiry* **12** 373–418.

McCarthy, John J. 1988. Feature geometry and dependency: a review. *Phonetica* **45** 84–108.

McCarthy, John J. 1989. Linear order in phonological representation. *Linguistic Inquiry* **20** 71–99.

McCarthy, John J. and Alan Prince 1986. Prosodic morphology, Ms, UMASS Amherst and Brandeis U..

McCarthy, John J. and Alan S. Prince 1990. Foot and word in prosodic morphology: The Arabic broken plural. *Natural Language and Linguistic Theory* **8** 209–283.

Mester, Ralf-Armin 1986. *Studies in tier structure*. PhD Thesis, UMASS Amherst.

Mester, Ralf-Armin 1990. Patterns of Truncation. *Linguistic Inquiry* **21** 478–485.

O'Shaughnessy, Douglas 1987. *Speech Communication, Human and Machine*. Addison Wesley.

Odden, David 1986.   On the role of the Obligatory Contour Principle in phonological theory. *Language* **62** 353–383.

Odden, David 1988.   Anti Antigemination and the OCP. *Linguistic Inquiry* **19** 451–476.

Pelletier, Francis J. 1980.   The generative power of rule orderings in formal grammars. *Linguistics* **18** 17–72.

Poser, William J. 1990.   Evidence for foot structure in Japanese. *Language* **66** 78–105.

Prince, Alan S. 1983.   Relating to the grid. *Linguistic Inquiry* **14** 19–100.

Ringen, Catherine O. 1976.   Vacuous application, iterative application, and the unordered rule hypothesis. In *The Application and Ordering of Grammatical Rules*, Andreas Koutsoudas, (ed.) Mouton, The Hague, 55–75.

Ringen, Catherine O. and Miklós Kontra 1989.   Hungarian neutral vowels. *Lingua* **78** 181–191.

Sagey, Elisabeth 1988.   On the ill-formedness of crossing association lines. *Linguistic Inquiry* **19** 109–119.

Salomaa, Arto 1973.   *Formal Languages*. Academic Press, New York.

Schabes, Yves 1991.   An inside-outside algorithm for estimating the parameters of a hidden stochastic tree-adjoining grammar, ms, University of Pennsylvania.

Schein, Barry and Donca Steriade 1986.   On geminates. *Linguistic Inquiry* **17** 691–744.

Selkirk, Elisabeth O. 1984.   *Phonology and Syntax: The Relation Between Sound and Structure*. MIT Press, Cambridge MA.

Selkirk, Elizabeth O. 1982.   *The syntax of words*. MIT Press, Cambridge MA.

Vágó, Robert M. 1980.   *The Sound Pattern of Hungarian*. Georgetown University Press.

Vogel, Irene and István Kenesei 1987. The interface between phonology and other components of the grammar: the case of Hungarian. *Phonology* **4** 243–263.

Wiebe, Bruce 1992. *Modelling autosegmental phonology with multitape finite state transducers*. MS Thesis, Simon Fraser University.

Williams, Edwin 1976. Underlying tone in Margi and Igbo. *Linguistic Inquiry* **7** 463–84.

Yip, Moira 1988. The Obligatory Contour Principle and phonological rules: a loss of identity. *Linguistic Inquiry* **19** 65–100.

Zwicky, Arnold M. 1992. Some choices in the theory of morphology. In *Formal grammar: theory and implementation*, Robert D. Levine, (ed.) Oxford University Press, 327–371.

Chapter 3

Duration

So far we have learned what autosegmental representations are (chapter 1) and how they are manipulated by autosegmental rules (chapter 2). But what is the point of all this manipulation? What are the representations produced by the rule systems good for? The received view in generative phonology is that the 'surface phonological representations' output by the phonological component serve as the input to a phonetic component which will produce an articulatory or acoustic specification from these. In other words, the meaning of phonological representations is to be found in their phonetic interpretation. Our aim here and in the next chapter will be to explicate this idea using the same formal mechanism that is generally used in logic and linguistics to explicate meaning, namely *model-theoretic semantics*.

The key idea of model-theoretic semantics is to specify a mapping, the *interpretation function*, which links the theoretical structure under investigation to actual structures that can be found in (platonic) reality. In order to make use of this idea in phonology we need three things: a specification of the *domain* of the interpretation function, a specification of its *range*, and a specification of the *mapping* itself. So far we have dealt with the domain, which is the set of well-formed autosegmental structures (see 1.1-1.3) and its temporal structure, which is given in terms of timing units (see 2.4.4). In this chapter we will deal with the range and its temporal structure, and with the real-time aspect of the mapping linking the two.

Phonologists generally view the task of phonetic interpretation as a procedure yielding the articulatory (or possibly acoustic) specification of a single prototypical utterance, perhaps parameterized for the physical dimensions that determine the speaker's idiosyncratic pitch range, vocal tract characteristics, and other biologically determined factors. Since explicitly specifying such an interpretation procedure is, as every speech engineer working on synthesis systems knows so well, a task of immense complexity, here attention will be shifted from the single prototypical utterance to the statistical ensembles of *all* utterances that can be the phonetic interpretation of a given surface phonological representation.

At first sight this might appear to be a more ambitious undertaking; for example, to specify the phonetic interpretation of vowel length we needed only one value (the duration of the prototypical vowel) under the generally accepted view, while under the view presented here we need to specify a *random variable* that assigns a duration value to each member of the statistical ensemble of vowel utterances. But as we shall see, it is in fact much easier to describe an interpretation function that maps representations onto model structures containing random variables than to include in the interpretation function all factors that contribute to the variability of speech. It is by now a commonplace in speech engineering that phoneticians in fact do not have a full understanding of the factors underlying the observed variability of speech, and that *ignorance models* (in the sense of Makhoul and Schwartz 1986) which capture the variability by statistical optimization techniques do much better than models based on human expertise.

This work attempts to bridge the gap between the practice of pho-nologists and the practice of speech engineers, and the key technical step in this undertaking is choosing model structures which on the one hand preserve the essence of the linguistic idea that phonological representations are to be interpreted as (parameterized) utterances and on the other hand are compatible with the speech engineering idea of determining parameters by statistical analysis (training). While the need for some kind of *phonetic structures* that can serve as models for interpreting autosegmental notation was recognized from the outset, the existing models, such as the *event structures* of Bird and Klein 1990, suffer from a serious deficiency: they are incapable of capturing the real-time nature of speech. The apparatus of temporal logic used in these investigations (see van Benthem 1983) is sufficient only for gross temporal relations, such as overlap and precedence, which are preserved by time warping. Since speech recognition applications demand a less abstract view, here I will concentrate on the real-time effects that are not warping-invariant. These aspects, primary among them the *duration* of phonological events, are only expressible in a formalism like the *metric temporal logic* of Koymans 1990 which contains an explicit notion of *distance* between points in time.

In order to establish the overall properties of segmental duration I will take theories, rather than data, as my starting point. The *classical* theory of duration, implicit in the vast majority of the experimental work on duration from Meyer 1903 to Klatt 1976 and beyond, is explicated in section 3.1. The *gestural* theory of duration developed at Haskins Labs (Browman et al. 1984, Kelso and Tuller 1987, Browman and Goldstein 1990a) is discussed in section 3.2. The lognormal hypothesis found to be implicit in these theories is used in section 3.3 to guide the reanalysis of the data of Crystal and House 1982. The implications of the results for phonetic interpretation in general, and Markov modeling in particular, are discussed in section 3.4, where the durational properties of the most important Hidden Markov topologies are analyzed, and *input* models are shown to be trainable to any prescribed duration density. This result is then used in 3.5 to justify the idea of using Markov models as the model structures in specifying the semantics of segmental duration.

3.1   The classical theory

In this section I investigate the "classical" theory of duration by means of
looking at a formally defined version due to Dennis Klatt (for a detailed
exposition, see Allen, Hunnicutt and Klatt 1987) from a rather abstract
point of view, and deducing predictions (e.g. shifted lognormal distribution of duration densities) on the basis of this formal definition, rather
than on the basis of measurements.   Whether my dubbing the theory
"classical" is justified or not is debatable, but I believe that the term is
correct inasmuch as the fundamental assumption underlying the model,
namely that the observed variability of segmental duration can be analyzed as the compound effect of various contexts (and overall tempo) on
the inherent duration of the segment, seems to be shared by nearly every
20th century phonetician/speech engineer.

To fix ideas, in this chapter utterances will be viewed as being composed of smaller units, such as phonological words, syllables, and segments in an exhaustive, non-overlapping manner.   Within every layer
of the hierarchy, each unit begins exactly the moment the previous
one ends, i.e. there is no overlap between the production/perception
of neighboring units.[1] By the phonemic principle each phone belongs to
one of a small number of language-particular equivalence classes called
phonemes. However, phonemes are defined as minimal contrastive units,
not as maximal homogeneous intervals, so we must leave open the possibility that a single phone is composed of a succession of more uniform
subphones (or *microsegments* such as a stop closure and a stop burst,
see e.g. Fant 1973). Here we assume that subphones are also strictly
concatenative – the issue of fuzzy boundaries will be taken up in chapter 4.

Let us denote the duration of a phone p_i, belonging to some phoneme
P_j, by $d(p_i)$. The numerical value of $d(p_i)$ will not, of course, be fully

---

[1]For a fuller discussion of the hierarchy of units relevant for phonology, see e.g. Nespor
and Vogel 1986, and for a clear statement of the alternative view, namely that phone-sized
units (and therefore larger units as well) generally overlap one another and there is no clear
partitioning of the utterance into intervals corresponding to segments, see e.g. Fowler and
Smith 1986.

determined by the phoneme or phoneme variant[2] p_i belongs to; it will be influenced by overall speech tempo (which in turn depends on the speech style, and even the emotional state, of the speaker), by the segmental and hierarchical context of the p_i token and perhaps by other, not readily identifiable factors. It is therefore reasonable to treat $d(p_i)$ as a random variable, and to define the duration $d(P_j)$ of a phoneme as the expectation

$$(1) \qquad\qquad \sum_{p_i \in P_j} f_{p_i} E(d(p_i))$$

Here E stands for mean (expected value) and f_{p_i} are the relative frequencies of the variants p_i belonging to the phoneme P_j. In the simplest case, when a phoneme P_j has only one variant, the formula reduces to $E(d(p_i))$. In what follows, I will discuss primarily this simple case – the results will trivially generalize to the case where a phoneme has a number of variants.

The simplest way to account for the effect of speech tempo is to normalize by a factor that is characteristic of the overall tempo (Heinitz 1921). With this normalization in effect, the classical theory of duration assumes that the expectation $E(d(p_i))$ is an inherent property of segment type P_j. In other words, the *actual* duration $d(p_i)$ will be a function of some *inherent* duration E_j and some *corrective factors* $\Delta_{k,j}$ which depend on segmental and hierarchical context k and perhaps on other factors. Most of the experimental research on segmental duration can be recast in this framework as an inquiry as to the numerical values of E_j and the corrective factors $\Delta_{k,j}$. A more abstract, but still data-driven approach is taken by van Santen and Olive 1990, where attention is shifted from the actual numerical values to the determination of the exact range of k, and to the manner in which different factors $\Delta_{k,j}$ interact.

---

[2]The term *phoneme variant* is used here to denote those groups of phones within a phoneme which are characterized by a high degree of phonetic similarity. Ideally, a phoneme will have only one variant, but we often find variants such as tapped vs. trilled *r* which form phonetically coherent subgroups within the whole group constituting the phoneme.

The classical literature on the subject of segmental duration is full of statements of the form "vowels are lengthened by 20% in stressed syllables" or "segments are 20% shortened before a nasal". In fact, durational rules of speech synthesis, such as discussed in Baker 1979, Carlson and Granström 1986, Allen, Hunnicutt and Klatt 1987, tabulate INHDUR values (our E_j) and PRCNT changes (out $\Delta_{k,j}$) of these values in contexts k, j. In what follows, I will concentrate on this multiplicative structure of the classical model which, in Klatt's formulation, is enhanced to include an additive MINDUR parameter, inherent in each phoneme, that serves as a lower bound for the values $d(p_i)$ can take. Our starting point is the basic equation of the Klatt model:

$$\text{DUR}(p_i) - \text{MINDUR}(P_j) =$$
$$\Pi_{p_i \in k} \ \text{PRCNT}_{j,k} \ (\text{INHDUR}(P_j) - \text{MINDUR}(P_j))$$

It has been observed[3] that the distribution of segmental length becomes more and more characteristically normal, with decreasing variance, as we fix more and more of the factors, such as phonemic identity, segmental context, degree of stress, etc. that influence duration. The Klatt model abstracts away from the remaining variability by replacing this normal variable by one that can be thought of as uniformly distributed (over a very short interval determined by the precision of the arithmetic) or even degenerate (concentrated on a single point). But the exact nature of the underlying distributions is irrelevant: as long as there are a large number of independent factors k that play a role in the rules governing duration, for every phone these will be present (or absent) in a random manner, and we can appeal to the Central Limit Theorem and deduce that (DUR − MINDUR) will follow a lognormal distribution, i.e. that the distribution of $d(p_i)$ follows an upshifted lognormal law.

---

[3]By Olive (pc). I am also indebted to Jan van Santen for his comments and criticisms. Needless to say, my conclusions are not necessarily shared by them.

For such an appeal to be successful we need to demonstrate two facts: that there are enough rules to justify taking the limit (which, in a literal sense, would require infinitely many rules) and that the contexts that trigger the rules are truly independent. As for the number of contexts, an overview of the duration literature shows that at least thirty contexts must be considered. Without attempting an exhaustive listing, we can identify at least the following factors:

1. local speech tempo

2. phonemic identity

3. position in the metrical structure

4. position in the word

5. position in the utterance

6. segmental context

Here local speech tempo refers to the fact that word length grows subadditively in the number of syllables, i.e. that the more syllables a word has the shorter these become. This factor is to be distinguished from overall speech rate, which is not listed above because of the normalization assumption made earlier. Phonemic identity contributes at least a dozen factors and possibly more, depending on the feature analysis used in the analysis of phonemes. Position in the metrical structure refers to three independent factors: position of the segment in the onset/rhyme, position within the syllable and position within the metrical foot.[4] Position within the word and position within the utterance refer to edge effects, generally closeness to the end, rather than the beginning, of a word or utterance, cf. Selkirk 1986. Finally, segmental context refers to nearby segments, both tautosyllabic and heterosyllabic. Even if we pool the effects of segments

---

[4]The impact of higher metrical constituents, such as "superfeet" remains to be demonstrated.

belonging to the same major class, if only adjacent segments are considered, this gives at least six factors, and if two segments are considered on both sides, this gives at least twelve factors, because at least three major class features are necessary.

Needless to say, not all these factors are completely independent. If a segment is utterance final, it must also be word final. Phonotactic constraints can establish strong correlation between the phonemic identity of a segment and its neighbors. The major class features will largely determine the position of a segment within the onset or the rhyme. But by a suitable change of base the feature system can be made completely orthogonal; for instance, we could replace the intricacies of metrical structure by a single (perhaps even binary) factor of *stress*. The real issue is not the number of factors we start with, but rather the number of orthogonal factors we end up with. According to van Santen (pc) we need some seven (multivalued) factors to account for 80% of the variance in duration data; this makes it likely that at least twice as many factors would be needed to account for 90% of the variance, and four times as many to account for 95%. This suggests that the number of independent factors will be sufficiently large to justify the abstraction of looking at a finite sequence of rules as if it was infinite.

But even if we could account for 95% of the variance using a multiplicative model or could closely fit a shifted lognormal curve to the samples analyzed in the literature, this does not, by itself, prove the correctness of the model. Still, there are some weighty reasons to believe that the classical model of duration, as presented above, cannot be far off the mark. First of all, it fits the data reasonably well (though not nearly as well as we would like – see section 3.3 below). Second, it *is* the case that the empirical distribution of $d(p_i)$ will be zero for some minimal duration t_0 (with $t_0=3$ msec, for concreteness), independent of the particular method of measuring duration (kymogram, spectral analysis) chosen. It should be emphasized here that the lower bound for MINDUR[5] does not

---

[5]In the light of published data, 3msec is perhaps excessively cautious. For example, the smallest MINDUR value used in Allen, Hunnicutt and Klatt 1987:96 is 20 msec.

depend on the inherent precision of the measurement, which is in the .1 msec range, but rather on the inherent impossibility of recognizing any "overshort" stretch of speech as belonging to any phoneme. In other words, the instruments are sensitive enough, but the *physiological* notion of a "phone" is not; for example, it simply makes no sense to speak of a vowel phone shorter than a single pitch period.

There is no doubt that psychologically a phoneme can be perceived even where all primary articulation is missing, just on the basis of secondary clues such as compensatory lengthening, nasalization, or formant movement in adjacent segments. However, the temporal span of such coarticulatory effects does not provide the missing segment with temporal extent for the simple reason that the phone carrying the coarticulation has its own temporal extent which it does not relinquish. (To use a simple spatial analog to the temporal situation that obtains, let us take a tightly packed bag of groceries. When I remove a banana showing the unmistakable signs of having been next to a pineapple, I will conclude that there was a pineapple next to this banana at some earlier time. I can even infer the size of this pineapple from the pattern it left on the banana. However, I cannot draw a conclusion as to how much space this pineapple now occupies in the grocery bag, for it might have crushed the banana back at the store, and it might not be present in the grocery bag at all.)

Another justification of MINDUR comes from the linear, but not homogeneous relationship between the duration of short and long vowels established by Fant and Kruckenberg 1989. In Swedish, at least, the average duration (in milliseconds) of long stressed vowels and short stressed vowels is related by a regression $V_{long} = 1.9V_{short} - 45$ as overall tempo ranges from connected speech to words spoken in isolation. If there was no MINDUR parameter, we would expect the average duration of long stressed vowels to be exactly twice as large as that of short stressed vowels, with the difference between the predicted 2 and the observed 1.9 perhaps attributable to *local* tempo effects. But there would be no reason to assume that a 45msec constant enters the equation, this makes sense only if there are MINDUR parameters present in the equations describing the relationship of vowel duration to overall tempo.

3.2   The gestural theory

The classical model, as embodied in the synthesis algorithm of MITalk, is deterministic: its ultimate justification comes not from good fit with duration measurements but from the quality of duration synthesis it produces. But it was almost trivial to peel off the deterministic layer (which is necessarily present in any algorithm) to reveal the key feature of the underlying probabilistic model, namely the multiplicative effect of independent factors. In this section I will analyze another deterministic model, the gestural theory developed at Haskins Labs (Browman and Goldstein 1989, Browman and Goldstein 1990b) with the aim of identifying the sources of variability according to the model.

The basic assumption of gestural theory is that speech production can be described in terms of successive and parallel gestures, with any single gesture corresponding to the "formation (and release) of a characteristic constriction within one of the relatively independent articulatory subsystems of the vocal tract" (Browman and Goldstein 1989:201). The unfolding of a single gesture is a solution to a second-order linear differential equation corresponding to a mass-spring model:

(2) $mx''(t) + bx'(t) + k[x(t) - x_0] = 0$

In the Haskins model, damping is set to critical, mass is normalized to unity, and the only parameters subject to variation across gestures, contexts, and individuals, are the *stiffness* k and the *displacement* x_0. Given these assumptions, the solutions to (2) are given by:

(3) $x(t) = (C_0 + C_1 t)e^{-\sqrt{k}t} + x_0$

The attainment of target position is defined in terms of the natural frequency of the system, as 2/3 of a full cycle:

> Because it takes an infinite amount of time to actually reach
> the target in a critically damped system, we have specified
> that the effective achievement of the target is at 240 degrees
> with respect to the abstract underlying 360 degree cycle.
> (Browman and Goldstein 1987:7)

If stiffness, like many other biological parameters that can only take positive values, is distributed lognormally (see Johnson and Kotz 1970 Ch 14.6), the time required to attain the target, which is given by

(4)
$$\frac{4\pi}{3}\frac{1}{\sqrt{k}}$$

will also be lognormally distributed. (Similarly, if log stiffness is distributed uniformly, log duration will also be uniformly distributed, and the same conclusion would hold for any family of distributions closed under linear transformations.) This prediction is directly relevant only for those segments which can be assumed to employ a single gesture (e.g. simple vowels). However, it can be easily extended to segments requiring multiple gestures, because the model defines the relative timing of such gestures in terms of phase angles. Therefore, in such cases the theory predicts duration to be the sum of lognormally distributed variables.

3.3   A statistical study

The lognormal hypothesis that emerged from the theories discussed so far encompasses a broad range of models. We have a choice between three-parameter and two-parameter lognormal distributions, i.e. we can investigate the model with or without MINDUR. For segments such as stops, where the decomposition into several subphones/gestures is justifiable, we could use the sum of lognormals, and for segments such as liquids where different phoneme variants can be assumed, we could use a mixture of lognormals. Furthermore, these families of lognormal models should be compared to the corresponding normal families, gamma families, and so on.

At this point it seems natural to proceed by analyzing a data set according to these hypotheses and applying statistical criteria to judge the goodness of fit. But before we do this, a word of caution is in order. Unless we deal with a finite domain, no amount of data is ever sufficient to establish positive results. It is certainly possible to find out which of two models fits the observations better. But it is not within the power of statistical analysis to *create* a model: models are created by humans capable of formulating hypotheses about the causal mechanism behind the observed data. To give an example, the careful and sophisticated exploratory data analysis presented in van Santen and Olive 1990 will certainly convince the reader that among the models they considered,

$$log(DUR) = f_1(id)f_2(rate)f_3(loc) + f_4(stress, loc)$$

describes the patterns in the data best. But why take the logarithm, rather than, say, the arcus tangent, of duration data? There is an infinite variety of functions to consider, and ultimately our goal is not to establish an empirical law that is expressible in terms of the more commonly used functions, but to understand the mechanism responsible for the observed phenomena. Statistical analysis is a powerful tool for comparing (and rejecting) empirical laws, but it loses its power when it comes to explanation.

With this caveat, let us now turn to the analysis of a rather detailed data set, kindly provided to the author by House (pc). The goals of this analysis are rather modest: we would like to establish the fact that the lognormal hypothesis is superior to the normal hypothesis, and conclude from this that a multiplicative model is superior to an additive one. Over 10,000 measurements from the "Hunter" and "Farm" scripts (see Crystal and House 1982) are summarized in the following table:

Table 1.

CH	N	MIN	MAX	MEAN	STD	SKEW	K
aa	247	47	322	134.3	42.7	0.9448	2.2752
ae	217	21	324	130.9	60.3	0.5215	-0.2328
ah	294	26	213	87.6	36.7	0.8165	0.3797
ao	167	37	318	146.0	57.8	0.6796	0.1958
aw	121	78	395	201.6	56.2	0.7442	0.7537
ax	413	7	198	49.2	17.0	2.3963	15.6174
ay	242	55	371	160.0	57.5	0.7692	0.7020
b	165	20	163	69.5	26.4	0.4982	0.3983
ch	77	53	222	126.6	36.0	0.6323	0.2243
d	158	16	187	72.4	24.9	0.5288	1.9931
dh	395	9	140	35.4	17.1	1.3957	3.8906
dx	153	9	72	30.0	11.0	1.0036	1.2641
eh	358	26	204	81.9	38.3	1.0414	0.7009
er	125	40	312	130.9	59.9	0.7260	-0.0092
ey	196	40	390	132.7	49.3	1.8027	6.0673
f	234	13	195	92.7	33.3	0.3635	0.1704
g	52	48	129	84.4	19.9	0.2819	-0.6588
hh	218	11	186	55.6	29.0	1.3526	3.0132
ih	674	9	159	59.7	24.9	1.0330	1.3809
in	23	34	162	88.0	29.2	0.3887	0.8587
ix	30	20	121	60.6	26.6	0.7564	-0.3247
iy	272	24	301	107.0	43.5	1.2557	2.5328
jh	45	59	176	105.1	31.4	0.7458	-0.5627
k	240	31	233	107.3	35.1	0.4256	-0.1259
l	395	25	205	71.2	27.9	1.2887	2.9937
m	305	15	165	71.2	24.7	0.8491	1.1586
n	653	18	218	64.6	28.4	1.6292	4.1849
nx	72	36	253	91.0	41.4	1.7171	3.5809
ow	122	65	340	155.0	61.3	1.0154	0.5446
p	59	45	174	101.5	26.7	0.1283	-0.1351
r	448	15	227	74.6	34.3	1.3503	2.8404
s	528	25	202	99.2	34.0	0.2058	-0.3224
sh	72	69	198	125.8	27.3	0.5255	0.0344
t	445	31	183	83.3	27.2	0.6961	0.3846
th	88	17	184	77.4	34.1	0.4241	-0.0194
uh	120	22	203	68.7	34.4	1.8762	4.0174
uw	108	36	309	113.6	53.4	1.5469	2.2509
ux	21	45	332	137.7	77.4	1.3221	1.0589
v	158	21	114	54.3	18.9	0.9941	0.9396
w	359	9	149	61.8	26.8	0.6065	-0.2206
y	59	19	160	56.9	25.4	1.3751	3.3729
z	359	21	210	67.2	26.0	1.6586	4.7250

Here and in Table 2 CH identifies the segment in darpabet notation. N is the number of tokens – in the case of stops only those with full hold and release portions are included here. MIN, MAX, and MEAN durations, as well as STD (standard deviation) values are given in milliseconds. Skewness (SKEW) and kurtosis (K) are sample, rather than population values.

For the sake of completeness, let me include here in Table 2 those segment types that only have a handful of tokens, as well as pause (pa) and silence (si) durations. In the following discussion, these will be ignored.

Table 2.

CH	N	MIN	MAX	MEAN	STD	SKEW	K
il	3	84	140	109.3	28.3	0.9147	0.0000
im	7	28	84	59.4	17.6	-0.5023	0.8394
oy	6	229	368	297.6	53.1	0.1141	-1.2723
q	5	13	46	26.0	13.7	0.8792	-0.9204
wh	3	23	85	52.1	31.4	0.7296	0.0000
pa	220	16	2362	375.6	293.0	2.0612	9.5819
si	217	10	4735	838.3	510.2	2.7655	16.6205

Clearly, the overall shape of shifted lognormal distribution has the same gross properties as the samples, as can be seen from the first few empirical moments. Length measurements always yield an empirical distribution with a heavy tail: the number of tokens with duration above the mode will be in excess of the number of tokens with duration below the mode. This becomes very conspicuous when compared to the prediction made by normal distribution (i.e. the assumption that context effects on length are additive, rather than multiplicative). The assumption of normality (Zwirner and Zwirner 1936) implies that the distribution of length is symmetrical around the mean. But because the mean does not coincide with the mode, no sample ever follows this law near the mean. And of course no sample ever follows this law away from the mean, because 0 is an absolute lower limit and there is no absolute upper limit on the length of segments.

On the other hand, there are several important distributions, most notably the gamma, that will have the same gross shape after the addition of a constant MINDUR, so not even an excellent fit with the data can properly justify the choice of lognormal distribution, especially as (1) makes it clear that in principle we must deal with a *mixture* of upshifted lognormal densities. But even if we leave this complication aside, we have to deal with a 3-parameter family, and only the means E_j and the variances D_j can serve as a basis for a straightforward estimate of the relevant parameters (mean and variance) of the upshifted lognormal distribution. In particular, the estimation of MINDUR (the upshift constant) remains problematic. In what follows, I will primarily compare the 2-parameter lognormal family with the normal family, and discuss the 3-parameter curves only in passing.

The fact that normal curves do not fit our data well can be easily established by considering the error induced by the negative values of the normally distributed variable: for a population that contains no negative values this will be negligible only if the mean is at least three times larger than the standard deviation. Since only a few segments *(aa aw ch g in jh k p sh t)* meet this simple test, the normal hypothesis can be safely disregarded. Similarly, if these samples were drawn from a normal population, we would expect skewness and kurtosis values close to zero – as Table 1 clearly shows, this is not what we find. The fact that (two-parameter) lognormal curves fit the data much better can also be established easily: both the chi-square and the Kolmogorov-Smirnov tests support this conclusion. Table 3 summarizes the chi-square and KS results for the original data and its logarithm:

Table 3.

CH	N-CHI	LN-CHI	N-KS	LN-KS	3-CHI	THR
aa	340.17	18.87	728	713	18.79	4
ae	35.52	20.62	899	903	20.62	0
ah	41.00	7.26	922	403	7.26	0
ao	8.41	7.08	715	601	7.08	0
aw	54.09	11.96	801	508	11.45	31
ax	1198.14	415.53	878	355	76.82	6
ay	49.70	11.90	783	561	11.90	0
b	26.25	12.26	498	931	12.26	0
ch	9.10	4.25	765	426	4.16	15
d	318.49	25.69	437	857	22.75	5
dh	150.32	17.14	1123	536	17.14	0
dx	39.88	3.52	965	325	3.45	2
eh	121.30	16.45	991	345	12.96	12
er	19.09	9.55	872	872	9.55	0
ey	2695.66	13.01	1119	698	10.21	19
f	16.14	43.77	406	869	43.77	0
g	3.95	3.04	845	725	3.03	9
hh	211.98	15.32	810	666	15.32	0
ih	233.30	11.84	887	312	11.84	0
in	2.19	1.95	1424	1447	1.95	0
ix	7.18	4.45	1767	1007	4.43	3
iy	238.63	8.34	743	311	8.28	4
jh	13.88	9.30	1621	1316	7.91	52
k	27.04	16.11	649	676	16.11	0
l	2423.26	11.57	910	252	10.87	4
m	79.83	16.68	850	438	16.68	0
n	44457.82	27.17	953	318	9.38	15
nx	106.17	6.50	1477	673	2.30	31
ow	38.27	10.48	1172	736	4.41	57
p	1.65	5.76	821	1067	5.76	0
r	630.12	13.95	781	404	13.95	0
s	4.51	1.50	368	740	1.45	13
sh	8.79	37.73	1019	610	37.73	0
t	4.39	6.45	784	353	6.45	0
th	39.30	6.29	636	898	6.29	0
uh	325.62	31.96	1656	749	11.98	21
uw	82.99	13.06	1718	995	5.18	31
ux	8.98	3.16	2072	1062	2.31	35
v	61.30	11.79	1015	377	9.31	12
w	43.85	17.31	879	586	17.31	0
y	26.70	3.38	1090	775	2.54	14
z	17294.24	22.05	1181	499	17.91	12

As in Table 2 CH identifies the segment in darpabet notation. N-CHI and LN-CHI give the chi-square values for the normal distribution and the lognormal distribution. N-KS and LN-KS give 10^4 times the Kolmogorov-Smirnov values. For 3-CHI and THR see below.

For the overwhelming majority of segment types, both the chi-square and the KS scores improve as we replace normal by lognormal. There are some exceptions (*f p sh t* for chi-square and *ae b d f in k p s th* for KS), but the overall tendency is very clear – we can safely conclude that a multiplicative model is better than an additive one. But the fit of the lognormal model is still rather bad, and does not improve really significantly if we add the third parameter.

Because of the numerical instability problems mentioned above (for a fuller discussion, see Aitchison and Brown 1957, Cohen 1988) no three-parameter curve fitting was attempted. Rather, the third parameter (the threshold value) was systematically varied between 0 and the smallest observation for each phoneme, with the other two parameters fitted, and the threshold yielding the best chi-square value was selected. The results of this theoretically questionable, but practically quite robust optimization method are summarized in the last two columns of Table 3 above: 3-CHI is the optimal chi-square value, and THR is the corresponding threshold (MINDUR) parameter. As Table 3 shows, the addition of a MINDUR parameter improves the chi-square values only in little more than half of the cases (23 out of the 42 considered), and only in a few cases is the improvement very pronounced. Nonetheless, the resulting MINDUR values are not unrealistic.

In conclusion, the lognormal model justified above on the basis of limit considerations clearly does not have enough parameters to account for the extreme variability present in duration data – in fact the variability is strong enough to make anything beyond the simple conclusion that multiplicative is better than additive hard to prove. One can assume, following van Santen (pc), that the reason for this is that the first few factors governing duration account for a disproportionately large share of the variance, so that later factors simply do not have the impact that would be necessary to homogenize the distribution.

Be that as it may, the multiplicative effect is still strong enough to call for an explanation. In section 3.2 above we have seen such a highly specific explanation of the underlying mechanism in terms of the dynamics of speech production; here I will sketch a less specific, but no less plausible explanation in terms of speech perception. We will need three assumptions. First, that segmental duration is proportional to the overall energy of a segment. This is trivially true for segments such as sonorants that can be said to be dominantly steady state, and is probably a reasonable approximation for obstruents as well. Second, that the psychological intensity of a stimulus is proportional to log energy (Weber-Fechner law). Third, that the psychological intensity of speech sounds is normally distributed. From these assumptions it follows by the definition of lognormality that duration will be lognormally distributed. However, it remains to be seen whether the third assumption has to be stipulated or can be shown by independent means.

3.4   Duration in Markov models

The inherently variable nature of speech production, rather strikingly demonstrated by the duration data discussed above, would be lost if the interpretation function mapped autosegmental structures onto metric event structures deterministically. Thus we are led to the conclusion that the range of the mapping should involve random variables; in the case of timing units, these should be mapped on duration variables, rather than directly on time intervals of definite length. If we had a good model of the factors involved in duration, each of these variables could be chosen to be defined by a few parameters that could be explicitly calculated from other aspects of the representation in question, such as the featural composition of the segment and its neighbors, and from overall parameters, such as speech rate and speaker-dependent parameters, that are not part of the representation but could be added to it at the point of phonetic interpretation. Unfortunately, we do not have a good model of the factors involved in duration, so we can not specify the parameters of the distributions; all we have is the rather abstract idea that timing units are mapped on random variables that take non-negative values which encode the durational aspects of the utterance. For the notion of interpretation function to make sense conceptually, this abstract idea is sufficient, because phonological representations abstract away from the actual content of the random variables anyway. But as a practical matter, we would like to find a compact way of capturing these random variables, preferably a way that will allow us to read off the distribution of the variables from the data directly. Such a compact representation is offered by Markov models, to which we turn our attention now. Here we will concentrate on the temporal aspect (topology and transition probabilities) of Markov models, and defer the discussion of their signal content until chapter 4.

Following Levinson, Rabiner and Sondhi 1983 I define a **Hidden Markov Model** (HMM) as a triple (π, A, B) where π is the *initial state distribution*, A is the matrix of *transition probabilities*, and B is the matrix of *signal distributions*. A single *run* of the model will start in some state i with probability π_i, where a signal v_j is emitted with probability $B_{i,j}$, and the model moves into state k with probability $A_{i,k}$ where another signal is emitted etc. In a word recognition task, each candidate word will have its own triple, and the recognition of a signal sequence $v_1 v_2 ... v_k$ is based on computing which triple could emit this sequence most probably.

In order to investigate the durational behavior of HMMs this generic scheme will be replaced by a more specific one in which HMMs correspond to single phones, rather than to full words. While in practice HMM recognizers always operate with mixed size units, often including clusters, syllables, full words and even combinations of words (Lee et al. 1990), in principle the durational characteristics of phone-in-context (triphone) models will make the dominant contribution as we move to more and more varied texts.[6] Therefore, the duration density of a single (allo)phone will be a mixture of the densities characterizing the triphone

---

[6]Strictly speaking, this need not be true in the case of segments like θ which are restricted to functions words like *that, than* which will have full word models anyway. In such cases, however, the HMM model actually makes no predictions as to the duration characteristics of the *segment* in question – the only prediction that is made concerns the duration of the whole function word.

models, assuming that the only context effect that is handled in the system is the influence of the adjacent segments.

In general, the same caveat has to be made concerning mixtures as in section 3.1 above: if the duration densities given by context-dependent models k are $d_k(t)$, and the probability of context k is f_k, the overall density will be given by

$$(5) \qquad\qquad d(t) = \sum_k f_k d_k(t)$$

Let us therefore concentrate on the case of a single phone in a fixed context. The single most crucial assumption I will make is that the succession of states $0,1,...,n$ in the HMM corresponds to the flow of time, i.e. if the model is in state i at time t_1 it cannot be in some other state $j < i$ for $t_2 > t_1$. (The possibility that the model remains in the same state for some period of time is left open, i.e. the transition probabilities $A_{i,i}$ are not assumed to be 0.) Given this "left-to-right" assumption (see section IV of Levinson, Rabiner and Sondhi 1983), the initial state distribution can be left out of consideration: we can simply say that state 0 is the *initial* and state n is the *final* state of the model.

3.4.1   The cascade model

The simplest model that corresponds with the flow of time is one in which state i will necessarily follow state $i - 1$, $(i = 1,..n)$. If we denote the time it takes to make a single transition by τ, any run will take exactly $n\tau$ time to arrive in the final state. A somewhat less trivial model is one in which state i follows state $i - 1$ only with probability $q < 1$, and the model can remain in state $i - 1$ with probability $p = 1 - q$. This makes a certain amount of time warping possible. The resulting model is called **cascade** following Crystal and House 1988:1566.

The cascade model, in spite of its striking simplicity, already has some highly desirable properties. First of all, it has a well-defined MINDUR $n\tau$ which is distinct from its INHDUR $n\tau/q$. Second of all, the time of arriving in the final state has Pascal (negative binomial) distribution (because advancing by a single state can be thought of as a Bernoulli trial – see Feller 1966. Ch 6.8.) which will show the required asymmetry. Therefore, it is worth looking into its behavior given an ideal computer which puts no limits on the number of states an HMM can have.

Clearly the granularity of the Pascal distribution will decrease with the time an elementary transition takes. In order to keep MINDUR and INHDUR constant, we can assume **contravariant timing**, i.e. that whenever we double the number of states in the model, we halve the execution time of an elementary step. As can be shown by the method of characteristic functions, the limiting distribution arrived at in this way will be concentrated on a single point, the expected value INHDUR.[7]

This result has rather striking practical consequences: it means that if transition probabilities are kept constant, increased frame rate can lead to decreased fit with the data! The alternative is to decrease the probability of self-loops as we increase the number of states, but this will converge only if we use **covariant timing** assuming that the time an elementary transition takes is proportional with the probability of this transition. While the limiting distribution arrived at this way is not unreasonable (we get Poisson density), the models used in this limiting process are, since the time it takes to traverse an arc will be different for different arcs.

3.4.2 The tridiagonal model

Perhaps the most frequently used variant of the Markov models embodying the left-to-right assumption is the **tridiagonal** model which permits not only self-loops and single transitions, but also double transitions or jumps from state i to state $i + 2$. Assuming that the probability of loops is p, the probability of a single step is q, and the probability of a jump is r, $(p + q + r = 1)$, the probability of a machine making exactly k moves to get from state 0 to state n is given by

---

[7] A more elementary demonstration of this fact can be based on the observation that as the parameter n is increased (and the parameter τ_n is proportionally decreased) the variance of the Pascal distribution will tend to 0.

(6) $\qquad\qquad\qquad\qquad\qquad\qquad\qquad\qquad p_n(k,p,q) =$

$$\sum_{w=0}^{n/2} [\frac{(k-1)!}{(k-n+1+w)!(n-2-2w)!w!}p^{k-n+1+w}q^{n-2-2w}r^{w+1}$$

$$+\frac{(k-1)!}{(k-n+w)!(n-1-2w)!w!}p^{k-n+w}q^{n-1-2w}r^{w+1}$$

$$+\frac{(k-1)!}{(k-n+w)!(n-1-2w)!w!}p^{k-n+w}q^{n-2w}r^w]$$

While this distribution is considerably more complex than the Pascal distribution associated with the cascade model, I will argue that in the limit the two are essentially the same, since again we get a distribution concentrated on a single point, namely the expectation $1/(q+2r)$. For a formal proof of this result and the other results announced without proof so far see the Appendix (section 3.6).

3.4.3   The input model

The equivalence of the **input** model and the **output** model (called "Type B topology" in Russell and Cook 1987) was noted in Crystal and House 1986. Input models are similar to the cascade model but they also contain transitions from the input state to any other state. The way these models will be investigated in the Appendix is by taking the initial state distribution π of cascade models to be adjustable; obviously the effect of starting in a random state is the same as the effect of starting in an initial state and than randomly jumping to some state. The final theorem in the Appendix shows that by a judicious choice of π we can fully control the duration density of the limiting distribution between 0 and $1/q$.

But the resulting density function will always be 0 for $t > 1/q$,[8] and this would be more adequate for distributions with a light tail. Still, if we are willing to stipulate the existence of a constant m (let's say, $m = 10$) such that no token longer than MAXDUR $= m \cdot$INHDUR is ever admitted,

---

[8]Without this requirement, we would be left with the physically unrealizable complex probabilities employed in Cox 1955.

we can use the input model (or the cascade model with nonuniform π) to model *any conceivable* duration density. Even with the stipulation of such a constant, this observation guarantees the convergence of the substitution approach discussed in Russell and Cook 1987 to train for duration by standard Markov techniques. Since $\int_0^\infty d(t)dt = 1$, we can choose MAXDUR so as to generate an error term $\int_{MAXDUR}^\infty d(t)dt < \epsilon/2$, and approximate $d(t)$ on the interval [0, MAXDUR] with error $< \epsilon/2$. This way, the total error of the approximation can be kept below any prescribed ϵ, making input models an ideal vehicle for expressing duration densities.[9]

3.5 Markov models as model structures

Let us now return to the idea we started out with at the beginning of this chapter, namely that the phonetic interpretation of autosegmental representations should involve statistical ensembles of utterances rather than single prototypical utterances. Now we are in a position to make this idea more precise as far as the phonetic interpretation of duration is concerned: the **segment-based interpretation function** maps autosegmental representations onto strings of left-to-right Markov models so that a separate Markov model corresponds to each root node in the representation.

There is no provision in this definition that root nodes with identical featural contents must be mapped on identical Markov models: for example, the first and the third Markov model in the interpretation of *bib* might be quite different. We will say that a model structure **durationally corresponds** with an autosegmental representation **to degree** ϵ if the observed duration density $o(t)$ of each segment (now restricted to the context provided by the representation) and the model's duration density $d(t)$ have L^1 distance $\int_0^\infty |d(t) - o(t)|dt < \epsilon$. *Content correspondence* can be defined analogously, using spectral distance measures.

---

[9]From a practical point of view, only models with a few states are really interesting. Although there is no guarantee that such models can approximate the actually obtaining duration densities to any degree, the results can be surprisingly good, especially as the transition probabilities of such models need not be kept uniform across states.

Before we generalize this idea to the autosegmental case in chapter 4, let us inspect it more closely from the model-theoretic semantic perspective. The basic idea is to explicate the meaning (semantics) of syntactically well-formed expressions by means of an interpretation function that maps such expressions onto the appropriately typed entities in model structures. In this case, the syntactically well-formed expressions are the segments and (as long as we abstract away from spectral content), the appropriate model structures are random duration variables, as expressed by Markov models. What is crucial here is that we do not map the (duration of) phonological entities such as segments directly onto stretches of utterances (having some definite duration). Rather, we create an indirect mapping: we map the segments onto random variables, which are themselves mappings from the set of segmental stretches of utterances to real numbers.

This way, the attention is shifted from the problem of ascertaining whether a single utterance token, or some stretch thereof, is an appropriate phonetic interpretation of the segmental representation to the larger but more interesting problem of ascertaining whether an *ensemble* of utterance tokens, endowed with the natural frequency-based probability measure, is an appropriate phonetic interpretation. Actually, we gain in simplicity by this shift in perspective because the random variables themselves can be thought of as accidental – only their distribution is relevant. It makes no difference whether the (duration) values come from measuring actual utterance tokens or from runs of appropriately designed Markov models, as long as the two have the same distribution. Given the result discussed in 3.4 above and proved at the end of the Appendix below that *any* duration distribution can be captured with arbitrary precision by Markov models with trainable input, we have a clear theoretical justification for using Markov models as model structures, since this specific choice of model structures results in no loss of expressive power[10].

---

[10]If spectral content is also taken into account, the completeness of Markov models becomes questionable – we return to this issue in chapter 5.

3.6 Appendix

In this section, I will first discuss the limiting distribution of duration density predicted by the tridiagonal model, and than show that the input model makes no comparable predictions. The reasons why the input model can yield any prescribed duration density distribution are elucidated in a way which is considerably more direct than the methods used in Cox 1955.

Given the structure of the tridiagonal model, its transition matrix A (except for the last two elements of the last column) can be written as $pI + qJ + rJ^2$, where I is the identity matrix and J has 1-s directly above the diagonal and 0-s elsewhere. In order to preserve the stochastic nature of the matrix, the row sums have to be set to 1 by taking $A_{n,n} = 1$ and $A_{n-1,n} = q + r$ – aside from this complication, the above decomposition holds. Notice that the matrix J is nilpotent: since it takes every base vector to the next one (except for the last one which it takes to 0), applying it $n + 1$ times will take every base vector to 0.

The probability of being in state j after k steps is given by $A_{1,j}^k$. The probability of being in state n after *exactly* k steps is r times the probability of being in state $n - 2$ after $k - 1$ steps plus $q + r$ times the probability of being in state $n - 1$ after $k - 1$ steps. (Recall that in order to preserve the stochastic nature of the matrix the probability of transition from state $n - 1$ to state n had to be taken as $q + r$.) This gives

(7)
$$p_n(k, p, q) = r A_{0,n-2}^{k-1} + (q + r) A_{0,n-1}^{k-1}$$

We can partition the transition matrix by splitting off the last column and the last row; this has no effect on the powers of A as far as values other than those of the last row and column are concerned, and in particular it leaves equation (7) unchanged. Therefore we no longer have to deal with the special transition probabilities of the last two states. In order to simplify the notation from now on the remaining top left submatrix will be denoted by A – for this the decomposition $pI + qJ + rJ^2$ is fully valid.

The $k - 1$st power of this matrix can be explicitly calculated: it is given by

(8) $$A^{k-1} = \sum_{u+v+w=k-1} \frac{(k-1)!}{u!v!w!} p^u q^v r^w J^{v+2w}$$

In order to evaluate (8) notice that only J^{n-2} will contribute to $A_{0,n-2}$ and only J^{n-1} will contribute to $A_{0,n-1}$. Therefore we have

(9) $$A^{k-1}_{0,n-2} =$$

$$\sum_{w=0}^{n/2} \frac{(k-1)!}{(k-n+1+w)!(n-2-2w)!w!} p^{k-n+1+w} q^{n-2-2w} r^w$$

and similarly for $A_{0,n-1}$. This gives

(10) $$p_n(k,p,q) =$$

$$\sum_{w=0}^{n/2} [\frac{(k-1)!}{(k-n+1+w)!(n-2-2w)!w!} p^{k-n+1+w} q^{n-2-2w} r^{w+1}$$

$$+ \frac{(k-1)!}{(k-n+w)!(n-1-2w)!w!} p^{k-n+w} q^{n-1-2w} r^{w+1}$$

$$+ \frac{(k-1)!}{(k-n+w)!(n-1-2w)!w!} p^{k-n+w} q^{n-2w} r^w]$$

Rather than working with this explicit distribution, it will be convenient to to use its generating function

(11) $$g_n(z) = \sum_{k=0}^{\infty} p_n(k,p,q) z^n$$

and later to collect these generating functions together in a two-variable generating function[11]

---

[11] This is what Wilf 1990 calls the "Snake Oil Method".

(12)
$$G(z,w) = \sum_{n=0}^{\infty} g_n(z) w^n$$

The crucial elements of equation (8) are the coefficients of J^{n-2} and J^{n-1} in the $k-1$st power of A – the equation is complicated because we expressed these coefficients from the trinomial expansion of the $k-1$st power of $A = pI + qJ + rJ^2$. However, if we use the matrix-generating function

(13)
$$T(z) = \sum_{k=0}^{\infty} A^k z^k$$

we can capture all these powers as

(14)
$$T(z) = [I - Az]^{-1}$$

(The use of the identity $\sum x^n = 1/(1-x)$ is justified because the eigenvalues of $x = Az$ are all $pz < 1$ for $z < 1/p$.) Using (11) we have

(15)
$$g_n(z) = \sum_{k=0}^{\infty} (rA_{0,n-2}^{k-1} + (q+r)A_{0,n-1}^{k-1}) z^k =$$
$$rzT(z)_{0,n-2} + (q+r)zT(z)_{0,n-1}$$

We can express $T(z)$ using only powers of J (recall that J is nilpotent) by solving

(16) $[(1 - pz)I - qzJ - rzJ^2][c_0 J^0 + c_1 J^1 + c_2 J^2 + ... + c_n J^n] = I$

which yields the Fibonacci-type recursion

(17)
$$c_{i+1} = c_i \frac{qz}{1 - pz} + c_{i-1} \frac{rz}{1 - pz}$$

with $c_0 = 1/(1 - pz)$, $c_1 = qz/(1 - pz)^2$. For a matrix of dimension n this recursion terminates with c_n, but as the initial two terms and the recursive definition are independent of n, we can use the same sequence of coefficients throughout.[12] The $k - 1$st power of A is given by the (matrix) coefficient of z^{k-1} in

$$(18) \qquad T(z) = \sum_{i=0}^{\infty} c_i(z) J^i$$

(For any fixed n, powers of J above n will be 0, but the notation is justified as the series is absolute convergent for e.g. $z < 1$.) In fact, we are interested only in the $n - 2$nd (and $n - 1$st) element in the 0th row of this matrix, and only J^{n-2} (and J^{n-1}) will contribute to these, so

$$(19) \qquad\qquad\qquad\qquad\qquad\qquad\qquad\qquad\qquad\qquad g_n(z) =$$
$$rzT(z)_{0,n-2} + (q+r)zT(z)_{0,n-1} = rzc_{n-2}(z) + (q+r)zc_{n-1}(z)$$

Using (14) with $i = n - 1$ this can be further simplified to

$$(20) \qquad\qquad g_n(z) = c_n(z)(1 - pz) + rzc_{n-1}(z)$$

for $n > 0$ (for $n = 0$ we set $g_0(z) = 1$). Recall that for the $c_i(z)$ we have a Fibonacci-type recursion that can be captured in the generating function

$$(21) \qquad F(z,w) = \sum_{n=0}^{\infty} c_n(z)w^n = \frac{\frac{1}{1-pz}}{1 - \frac{qz}{1-pz}w - \frac{rz}{1-pz}w^2}$$

Let us now investigate the two-variable generating function

$$(22) \qquad G(z,w) = \sum_{n=0}^{\infty} g_n(z)w^n = 1 + \sum_{n=1}^{\infty} g_n(z)w^n$$

Using (17) this yields

$$(23) \qquad G(z,w) = 1 + \sum_{n=1}^{\infty} (c_n(z)(1 - pz) + rzc_{n-1}(z))w^n$$

---

[12] Informally, we could enlarge the dimension of A indefinitely and partition this matrix so that we only consider the first $n - 1$ by $n - 1$ submatrix.

which, using (18), gives

$$G(z,w) = c_0(1-pz) + (F(z,w) - c_0)(1-pz) + rzwF(z,w) =$$
$$\text{(24)} \qquad \frac{1 - pz - rzw}{1 - pz - qzw - rzw^2}$$

If $r = 0$, this reduces to $\frac{1}{1-\frac{qz}{1-pz}w}$, which yields $g_n(z) = (\frac{qz}{1-pz})^n$, which is indeed the generating function of the Pascal distribution (cf. Feller 1966 ch XI.2.d). For any random variable X over the nonnegative integers, $g(1) = 1$, $g'(1) = E(X)$, and $g''(1) + g'(1) - g'^2(1) = D^2(X)$ (cf. Feller 1966 ch XI.1). Since the two-variable generating function $G(z,w)$ is rational by (24), in effect it contains all the information concerning the distributions $d_n(k,p,q)$ (because these numbers are the coefficients of $z^n w^k$ in its Taylor expansion). We can exploit this fact by finding the expectation and variance of the limiting distribution by asymptotic analysis. $G(z,w) = \sum_{n=0}^{\infty} g_n(z)w^n$ and thus

$$\text{(25)} \qquad \frac{rw + qw + rw^2}{(1 - pz - qzw - rzw^2)^2} = \frac{\partial G(z,w)}{\partial z} = \sum_{n=0}^{\infty} g_n'(z)w^n$$

so the asymptotic behavior of the nth coefficient $g_n'(1)$ is given by the behavior of $\frac{rw+qw+rw^2}{(1-p-qw-rw^2)^2}$ around its first pole in $w = 1$. Taking $x = 1 - w$ we get

$$\text{(26)} \qquad \frac{\partial G}{\partial z}\Big|_{1,1-x} = \frac{1-x}{x^2} \cdot \frac{1}{2r + q - rx}$$

meaning that the coefficient of the (second order) pole in the Laurent expansion around 1 is $1/(q + 2r)$. Therefore, the mean of the nth distribution is asymptotically $n/(q + 2r)$ and using contravariant timing the mean of the nth normed distribution is $1/(q + 2r)$. In fact the mean of the nth distribution is *exactly* $n/(q + 2r)$ as can be seen from the following argument.

In a single move, the model stays in the same state with probability p, advances by one state with probability q, and advances by 2 states with probability r. Therefore, on the average it will advance by $q + 2r$ states, and advancing n states will take on the average $n/(q+2r)$ steps. The only problem with this simple argument is that it does not generalize from the mean to higher moments – if we had a similar elementary argument for the variance, the whole function-theoretic apparatus of this Appendix could be dispensed with.

In order to establish the variance, let us differentiate $G(z, w)$ in z a second time. This gives

(27) $$\frac{\partial^2 G}{\partial z^2}\Big|_{1,1-x} = \frac{2(1-x)}{x^3}\frac{1-qx+rx^2-2rx}{(2r+q-rx)^2}$$

meaning that the coefficient of the (third order) pole in the Laurent expansion around 1 is $1/(q+2r)^2$. Therefore, the variance the nth distribution is asymptotically $n^2/(q+2r)^2+n/(q+2r)-n^2/(q+2r)^2 = n/(q+2r)$ and using contravariant timing the variance of the nth normed distribution is $1/n(q+2r) \to 0$.

For the special case $r = 0$, the result that the limit of the normed distributions is concentrated on the mean can be established directly. Recall that the generating function of the nth distribution was $g_n(z) = (\frac{qz}{1-pz})^n$ and therefore the characteristic function of the nth normed distribution is

(28) $$\chi_n(s) = \left(\frac{qe^{\frac{is}{n}}}{1-pe^{\frac{is}{n}}}\right)^n$$

If n tends to infinity, $e^{\frac{is}{n}}$ can be approximated by $1 + \frac{is}{n}$, which means that the base in (25) can be approximated by

(29) $$\frac{q(1+\frac{is}{n})}{1-p(1+\frac{is}{n})}$$

Dividing both the numerator and the denominator by q and applying the approximation $1/(1-z) \approx 1+z$ will yield

(30) $$\chi_n(s) \to (1+\frac{is}{qn})^n \to e^{\frac{is}{q}}$$

which is indeed the characteristic function of the distribution concentrated on the point $1/q$.

Finally, let us establish the theorem that the input model can be trained to any prescribed duration density distribution. If we assume uniform initial distribution, the probability of arriving in state n in the kth step is:

(31) $$p_n(k,p) = \frac{1}{n+1} \sum_{i=0}^{n} d_{n-i}(k-1,p)$$

For the generating function $h_n(z)$ we thus have

(32) $$h_n(z) = \frac{z}{n+1} \sum_{i=0}^{n} g_i(z) = \frac{z}{n+1} \frac{1-(qz/1-pz)^{n+1}}{1-(qz/1-pz)}$$

Again using contravariant timing, the characteristic function of the limiting distribution is

(33) $$\chi(s) = \lim_{n \to \infty} h_n(e^{\frac{is}{n+1}}) = \frac{q}{is}(e^{\frac{is}{q}} - 1)$$

which is the characteristic function of uniform distribution in $(0, 1/q)$.

In order to create a heavier tail, we can adjust the weights of the input distribution in favor of smaller input jumps: for instance, if the weights decrease linearly from $2/n$ to 0, the density function will increase linearly from 0 to $2q$ in the interval $(0, 1/q)$. This result can be generalized to any system of weights $w_n(i)$ that satisfy $\lim_{n \to \infty} n w_n(\lambda n) = f(\lambda)$ for some piecewise continuous function f in $0 < \lambda < 1$ because the weights act, in the limit, on impulse functions.

A more rigorous proof can again be based on characteristic functions. The generating function of the nth weighted sum will be equal to $z \sum_{i=0}^{n} w_n(n-i)g_i(z)$, so the characteristic function of the nth normed distribution will be $\frac{1}{n+1} \sum_{i=0}^{n} f(\frac{n-i}{n})(\frac{qe^{\frac{is}{n+1}}}{1-pe^{\frac{is}{n+1}}})^{(n+1)\frac{i}{n+1}}$ which tends to $\int_0^1 f(1-\lambda)e^{\lambda \frac{is}{q}} d\lambda$. By taking f to be 0 for $x < 0$ and $x > 1/q$ this is exactly a Fourier- Stieltjes transform of $f(1-\lambda)$, QED.

3.7   References

Aitchison, J. and J.A.C. Brown 1957. *The lognormal distribution.* Cambridge University Press.

Allen, Jonathan, M. Sharon Hunnicutt and Dennis Klatt 1987. *From text to speech: the MITalk system.* Cambridge University Press.

Baker, James K. 1979. Trainable grammars for speech recognition. In *Speech Communication Papers for the 97th Meeting of the ASA,* D.H. Klatt and J.J. Wolf, (eds.) 547–550.

Benthem, Johan van 1983. *The logic of time: a model-theoretic investigation into the varieties of temporal ontology and temporal discourse.* Kluwer Academic, Dordrecht.

Bird, Steven and Ewan H. Klein 1990. Phonological events. *Journal of Linguistics* **26** 33–56.

Browman, Catherine P. and Louis Goldstein 1987. Tiers in articulatory phonology with some implications for casual speech. *Haskins Laboratories Status Report* **SR-92**.

Browman, Catherine P. and Louis Goldstein 1989. Articulatory gestures as phonological units. *Phonology* **6** 201–251.

Browman, Catherine P. and Louis Goldstein 1990. Gestural specification using dynamically-defined articulatory structures. In *Journal of Phonetics.* to appear.

Browman, Catherine P. and Louis Goldstein 1990. Tiers in articulatory phonology with some implications for casual speech. In *Papers in Laboratory Phonology I: Between the Grammar and Physics of Speech,* John Kingston and Mary E. Beckman, (eds.) Cambridge University Press, 341–376.

Browman, Catherine P., Louis Goldstein, J.A.S. Kelso, P. Rubin and E. Salzmann 1984. Articulatory synthesis from underlying dynamics. *JASA* **75** S22–S23.

Carlson, Rolf and Björn Granström 1986. Swedish durational rules derived from a sentence data base. *Quarterly Progress and Status Report* **2-3** 13–25.

Cohen, A. Clifford 1988. Three-parameter estimation. In *Lognormal distributions*, Edwin L. Crow and Kunio Shimizu, (eds.) Marcel Dekker Inc., New York, 113–137.

Cox, D. R. 1955. A use of complex probabilities in the theory of stochastic processes. *Proc. Cambridge Pholosophical Society* **51** 313–319.

Crystal, Thomas H. and Arthur S. House 1982. Segmental durations in connected speech signals: preliminary results. *JASA* **72** 705–716.

Crystal, Thomas H. and Arthur S. House 1986. Characterization and modeling of speech-segment durations. In *ICASSP-86*. Tokyo, 2791–2794.

Crystal, Thomas H. and Arthur S. House 1988. Segmental durations in connected speech signals: current results. *JASA* **83** 1553–1573.

Fant, Gunnar 1973. *Speech Sounds and Features*. MIT Press, Cambridge.

Fant, Gunnar and Anita Kruckenberg 1989. Preliminaries to the study of Swedish prose reading and reading style. *Speech Transmission Laboratory – Quarterly Progress and Status Report* **2** 1–80.

Feller, William 1966. *An introduction to probability theory and its applications.* vol. 1, Wiley.

Fowler, Carol A. and Mary R. Smith 1986. Speech perception as vector analysis: an approach to the problems of invariance and segmentation. In *Invariance and Variability of Speech Processes*, Joseph S. Perkell and Dennis H. Klatt, (eds.) Lawrence Erlebaum Associates, Hillsdale, NJ, 123–136.

Heinitz, W. 1921. Die Bewertung der Dauer in phonetischen Aufnahmen. *Vox* **31**.

House, Arthur   pc.   Personal communication.

Johnson, N. L. and S. Kotz 1970.   *Distributions in Statistics: Continuous Univariate Distributions*. Houghton Mifflin, Boston.

Kelso, J.A.S. and B. Tuller 1987.   Intrinsic time in speech production: theory, methodology, and preliminary observations. In *Motor and sensory processes of language*, Eric Keller and Myrna Gopnik, (eds.) Lawrence Erlbaum, Hillsdale NJ, 203–222.

Klatt, Dennis H. 1976.   The linguistic uses of segmental duration in English: Acoustic and perceptual evidence. *JASA* **59** 1208–1221.

Koymans, Ron 1990.   Specifying real-time properties with metric temporal logic. *Real-Time Systems* **2** 255–299.

Lee, Kai-Fu, Hsiao-Wuen Hon, Mei-Yuh Hwang and Sanjoy Mahajan 1990.   Recent progress and future outlook of the SPHINX speech recognition system. *Computer Speech and Language* **4** 57–69.

Levinson, Stephen E., Lawrence R. Rabiner and M. M. Sondhi 1983. An introduction to the aplication of the theory of probabilistic functions of a Markov process to automatic speech recognition. *The Bell System Technical Journal* **62** 1035–1074.

Makhoul, John and Richard Schwartz 1986.   Ignorance modeling. In *Invariance and Variability of Speech Processes*, Joseph S. Perkell and Dennis H. Klatt, (eds.) Lawrence Erlebaum Associates, Hillsdale, NJ, 344–345.

Meyer, E. A. 1903.   *Englische Lautdauer*. Uppsala - Leipzig.

Nespor, Marina and Irene Vogel 1986.   *Prosodic phonology*. Foris, Dordrecht.

Olive, Joseph   pc.   Personal communication.

Russell, Martin J. and Anneliese E. Cook   1987.   Experimental evaluation of duration modelling techniques for automatic speech recognition, ICASSP, Dallas, TX.

Santen, Jan P.H. van and Joseph P. Olive 1990.   The analysis of contextual effects on segmental duration. *Computer Speech and Language* **4** 359–390.

Santen, Jan van   pc.   Personal communication.

Selkirk, Elisabeth O. 1986.   On Derived Domains in Sentence Phonology. *Phonology Yearbook* **3** 371–405.

Wilf, Herbert J. 1990.   *Generatingfunctionology*. Academic Press.

Zwirner, Eberhard and K. Zwirner 1936.   *Grundfragen der Phonometrie.* Metten & Co., Berlin.

Chapter 4

Synchronization

At this point, the formalization of autosegmental theory is nearly complete. We have developed a theory of autosegmental notation in chapters 1 and 2, and in chapter 3 we have presented the key idea of interpreting this notation, namely that the model structures appropriate for phonology are statistical ensembles of utterances to be captured in structures containing random variables. Here the example of segmental duration that we used for presenting this idea will be generalized to the autosegmental case. This further step is necessary because segments are not primitive units in autosegmental phonology, they are composed of partially overlapping features that unfold in time according to the synchronization provided by the association lines among them. Thus in order to complete the picture we need a theory of *synchronization* that tells us how to interpret features and the association lines among them.

Rather than presenting the formal definition of synchronization at the outset and proceeding deductively, we will build the formalism step by step, in an inductive manner. What are the model structures, and how do we map autosegmental representations on them? No doubt there will be readers who want to see the answers immediately. Yet the complexity of these notions is quite considerable, and it seemed best to choose the aesthetically less pleasing, but perhaps more effective,

inductive manner of presentation. First, in section 4.1 we examine the
notion of features and feature geometries informally (the results of a more
formal investigation are presented in the Appendix). Next we divide the
problem into two closely interrelated, but logically separate issues, *local*
and *global* interpretation.[1]

Local interpretation, reflecting the *microsynchrony* of articulatory
gestures, is the subject of section 4.2, where the notions of *phasepoints*
and *lag* are introduced. This is where the basic ideas of timing presented
in section 2.4.4 are related to the theory of features and feature geometry
by specifying the model structures and the interpretation of segments.
Global interpretation, reflecting the large-scale structural properties of
speech, but built compositionally from local interpretations, is the subject
of section 4.3.

4.1   What does feature geometry mean?

In order to formulate a theory of microsynchrony that maps autosegmental
representations composed of features on model structures of some sort,
it will be expedient to look at the ideas of autosegmental phonology
embodied in features and feature geometry from a broader perspective.
First we will look at two older conceptions of features, that of SPE
and that of Pāṇini, and then proceed to show that the modern theory
of feature geometry is more general than either of these. Using the
insights gained from this metatheoretical comparison, the model-theoretic
interpretation of segments will be presented in section 4.2, and that of
longer representations in section 4.3.

In a narrow sense, we already have the answer to the question of what
feature geometry means – it means that the tiers containing the features
that make up the representation of segments and larger units are arranged

---

[1]This division is made possible by the fact that the use of association lines between
features in autosegmental theory rests on two kinds of evidence: *subsegmental*, such as the
behavior of affricates, prenasalized stops, and other complex segments, and *suprasegmental*
such as the behavior of tonal melodies and harmony domains (for a concise overview, see
e.g. van der Hulst and Smith 1982).

in a (rooted) tree structure (see section 1.5). This formal, syntactic definition will later in this chapter be coupled with a formal, semantic definition that tells us how to interpret segmental structures conforming to some pre-defined feature geometry in models. Our goal here is to provide an answer in less formal, but, for the practicing researcher, more central, terms – how can features and feature geometries be used?

If we wish to characterize the phonological system of a language, we need to specify the segmental inventory S (defined broadly so as to include both underlying and surface phonemes) and some rules, either declarative or procedural, which specify the mapping between underlying and surface forms. For example, the nominative form of Russian nouns can be predicted from their dative forms by removing the dative suffix u and inspecting the final consonant; if it was b or p the final consonant of the nominative form will be p. This could be expressed in a purely segmental rule of *final b devoicing:*

(1) $$b \rightarrow p/\_\#$$

Most remarkably, we find that a similar rule links d to t, g to k, and in fact any voiced obstruent to its voiceless counterpart. This phenomenon, that the structural description and/or the structural change in rules will be met not only by a single segment, but rather by some bigger set of segments R, is in fact so pervasive that it makes a great deal of sense to introduce some formal apparatus that enables us to exploit it in our characterization of the phonological system. What is required is a clever notation that lets us characterize any such $R \subset S$, traditionally called a *natural class*, in a compact manner so that rules stated in terms of natural classes are just as easy, or perhaps even easier, to deal with as rules stated in terms of segments.

The set $N \subset 2^S$ of natural classes is not really under the control of the grammarian; it is externally given by the phonological patterning of the language. The notational devices that we use to capture natural classes are successful to the extent that they make it easier to use natural classes (i.e. members of N) than unnatural ones (i.e. those not in N) in the rules. Clearly, nothing can be won by expressing natural classes disjunctively in terms of their members, since this approach works for unnatural classes like $\{p, t, b\}$ just as well as it works for natural classes like $\{p, t, k\}$. What is needed is a more clever notation, such as the one provided by feature geometry, that exploits the internal structure of N to achieve notational compactness. Since feature geometry accomplishes this goal by rather complex means, first we will present two simpler notations aiming at compactness, and show that they are, in a well-defined sense, special cases of feature geometry.[2]

The two simple notations that we will consider here are the well-known "standard" (SPE) feature-based notation and the perhaps less widely known, but no less interesting interval-based notation employed by Pāṇini – let us take each in turn. Cherry 1956, Cherry 1957[3] describes the assignment of feature values to segments as a mapping from the set S into the Euclidean space of dimension n, where n is the number of features used in the analysis. Cherry conceives of this Euclidean space as being phonetic in nature – the coordinates correspond to physically measurable properties of the sounds such as formant values. In this work we take a slightly more complex technical route. The direct mapping between features and observables is replaced by two-stage mapping in which feature assignment is viewed as a phonemic, rather than phonetic, first step, and the resulting abstract structures (rooted trees) are interpreted phonetically in the second step. In keeping with the binary nature of phonological features, the underlying field of reals used by Cherry is replaced by the finite field GF(2).[4] Thus we define a **feature assignment**

---

[2]An algebraic investigation of the way feature geometry expresses natural classes is relegated to the Appendix (section 4.4), as it would take us far away from the central issue of motivating the model structures introduced in section 4.2.

[3]Since the use of distinctive features is fundamental to both classical (SPE) and modern (autosegmental) generative phonology, it is altogether remarkable that the best known formal model of features (see also Cherry, Halle and Jakobson 1953) actually predates generative phonology.

[4]There are only two elements in GF(2): 0 and 1. Arithmetic is performed in the usual way, except for the fact that 1+1=0.

as an injective mapping C from a given set S of segments $s_1, s_2, ..., s_k$ into the linear space GF(2,n). In other words, each segment is mapped on an n-tuple of 0s and 1s. At this stage of the analysis, no partially specified segments (archisegments) are permitted.

As we have discussed above, a clever feature assignment must be able to capture the natural classes defined by the phonological system of the language in a *notationally compact* manner. Following Halle 1964:328 those classes that can be expressed by fewer features than their individual members will be called **N-classes**. In GF(2,n) these are the hyperplanes parallel to the axes and their set will be denoted by N(2,n). A feature assignment C will be called **compact** if it maps sets in N onto $C(S) \cap N(2,n)$. If a compact feature analysis exists, it is easy to show that the following propositions are true:

(2) The number of natural classes is small – for $|S| = k$, $|N| \leq k^{1.58}$.
(3) The set of natural classes N must be basically closed under intersection – for $U, V \in N$, $s \in U, V$, either $U \cap V = \{s\}$ or $U \cap V \in N$.

Essentially the same two propositions follow from the first extant treatment of natural classes, given in Pāṇini 1.1.71. Simplifying matters somewhat (for a fuller discussion, see Staal 1962), Pāṇini's method is to arrange the phonemes in a linear sequence (the *śivasūtras*) with some indicatory letters *(anubandha)* interspersed. Natural classes *(pratyāhāra)* are defined as those subintervals of the *śivasūtras* which end in some *anubandha*. The number of *pratyāhāra* on k segments with p equidistant *anubandha* is $\approx k(p + 1)/2 \leq k(k + 1)/2$, again a small power (at most the square) of k. Furthermore, the intersection of two *pratyāhāra*, if not empty, can also be expressed as a *pratyāhāra*, and is, therefore, 'natural'.[5]

---

[5] In addition to using *pratyāhāra*, Pāṇini employs a variety of other devices, most notably, the concept of 'homogeneity' *(sāvarṇya)* as a means of cross-classification (see Cardona 1965). This idea, roughly corresponding to the autosegmental concept of a [supralaryngeal] class node, enables Pāṇini to treat quality distinctions in vowels separately from length,

So far we have seen two kinds of notations that enable the grammarian to refer not only to segments, but also to natural classes in the statement of phonological rules. In the standard theory, the savings come from the fact that only those features are mentioned which take the same value for each member of the natural class in question. For the Russian final devoicing rule mentioned above these features are [−sonorant] and [+consonantal] in the structural description, and [−voice] in the structural change of the rule. In the Pāṇinian theory the savings come from the fact that rather than referring to the whole set of obstruents, we only have to refer to the initial member and the closing anubandha of the class. What is common to both of these theories is that their evidence comes from the phonological domain – it is the phonological clustering of segments that determines feature assignment or anubandha placement.

The modern theory of features rests on Jakobson's fundamental insight that the phonological clustering of segments has a phonetic basis. As we shall see in chapter 5, the method of interpretation developed here makes it possible to exploit this fact for the construction of statistical models of speech. Feature geometry, when formulated abstractly, turns out to be a generalization of both the standard and the Pāṇinian approaches. The standard theory, based on feature vectors, gives rise to the finite linear space GF(2,n) which has Boolean algebraic structure. In the Appendix this will be generalized to feature geometries using the semi-independent boolean rings (SIBRs) introduced by Ehrenfeucht (pc). As we shall see shortly, in feature geometry the linear intervals of the Pāṇinian model are replaced by generalized (lattice-theoretic) intervals, meaning that the main source of generality in feature geometry is that it permits all kinds of rooted labelnode trees (see section 1.5), but only one of these, called the "paddle wheel" in Archangeli 1985, and the "rolodex" in Goldsmith 1990, is a notational variant of the standard model.

nasality, and tone distinctions, as well as to treat place of articulation distinctions in consonants separately from nasality, voicing, and aspiration contrasts. Another subsidiary concept, that of *antara* 'nearness', is required to handle the details of mappings between natural classes. Since the rules only map classes onto classes, the image of a segment under a rule is decided by 1.1.50 *sthāne 'ntaratamaḥ* 'in replacement, the nearest'.

To establish a one-to-one correspondence between the feature vectors
of the standard theory and the star-shaped trees in which all features are
daughters of the root node of the tree, consider an arbitrary set of n features
$f_1, ..., f_n$. If a segment has, say, value 1 (+) for features $f_1, ..., f_k$, and
value 0 (–) for $f_{k+1}, ..., f_n$, the corresponding 'geometrically arranged'
feature structure will have the nodes $f_1, ..., f_k$, and only these, dominated
by the root node. It is easy to see that the collection of feature structures
corresponding to an N-class will be a collection of substars all containing
some star B and contained in some larger star T. Since labeled graphs
form a distributive lattice for the usual set theoretic operations of union
and intersection, the elements of the N-class will thus correspond to a
(closed) *interval*, in the lattice-theoretic sense, between B and T. Every
interval of this sort will be called an **M-class**.

In the standard case, N-classes and M-classes coincide, and in the
case of more complex geometries, I will use M-classes to *define* what is
meant by 'compact notation'. (Given the Linking Constraint of Hayes
1986, this definition also accords with phonological practice in the case of
segments with branching root nodes like affricates and geminates, since
such complex segments can never fit the same structural description
or structural change as simplex segments[6].) As we shall see in 4.1.2
below, the use of M-classes enables us to view both ordinary segments
and archisegments as part of the same geometry, so that more complex
displays where a group of features is dominated by a single class node
can be reduced to two-tiered displays that have a much simpler geometry.

This concludes our discussion of the paradigmatic relations among
features. Before we turn to syntagmatic relations (linear ordering and
synchronization) below, the following remark is in order. Features, just
as segments, can be viewed as fuzzy units with no clear-cut temporal
boundary, or as sharply delimited, strictly concatenative units. In the

---

[6]If we maintain a theory of single-valued features throughout (see e.g. van der Hulst
1988), the notion of M-classes can be used to explicate the notion of natural classes without
the introduction of the coordinate system discussed above, but if we use two-valued features,
some kind of boolean apparatus must also be used, as we shall see in the Appendix.

rest of this work we will present the interpretation of feature structures from the strict perspective – it will be assumed that features have definite beginning and endpoints. But it should be emphasized that a strict view of features is compatible with a fuzzy view of segments, so much so that a strict view of features can actually serve as a basis for a formal reconstruction of the fuzzy view of segments. It has been recognized from the outset (Goldsmith 1976) that the framework of autosegmental phonology is based on a rejection of the Absolute Slicing Hypothesis; since features are placed on different tiers, there is no guarantee that all features in the bundle comprising the segment will begin or end simultaneously (see section 5.1). On the contrary, the expectation, which we will make more precise shortly, is that the features that make up a segment will begin at different points in time, so that the feature content characterizing a segment is manifested incrementally. While not fully fuzzy, this view entails that segments do not come into being in a single time instant, but rather they will manifest themselves gradually, possibly through as many stages as there are features.

4.2   Interval structures

To see how the interpretation mechanism works, we will proceed from the case of a simple binary feature node in the geometry to more complex class nodes which carry the explanatory burden of multivalued features. Let us first consider an undoubtedly binary feature such as [nasal]. In the feature geometry of Clements 1985, [nasal] attaches to [manner], which in turn attaches to [supralaryngeal], which in turn will attach to the root. But with an easy formal trick, we can reduce the case of indirectly attached features to the case of features directly attached to the root node.[7] In section 1.5 we defined the *content* of a leaf node in the geometry as the feature labeling of the node in question, e.g. [+nasal], and the content

---

[7]In fact, the feature [nasal] is attached directly to the root in McCarthy's (1988) version of feature geometry. But McCarthy uses substantive arguments to show that [nasal] *must* be located there, while here we use formal arguments to show how it can be *re*located there.

of internal nodes as the set of the contents of its daughters. Thus the content of a root node is what is traditionally called the featural content of a segment. The formal trick is to extend this idea to trees starting at the root but missing a subtree. For example, the content of a vowel node **modulo** nasality is defined as the archisegment composed of all those segments that share the featural content of the vowel, except possibly for the feature(s) dominated by the nasal node. Given the segmental inventory S, we can thus create a nasality-neutral inventory S/N, and express the segments in a two-tiered display, with one tier reserved for nasality and the other for nasality-neutral archisegments. Using this method of "currying" repeatedly, we can reduce the issue of interpreting any geometrical configuration of multi-tiered displays to the issue of interpreting two-tiered displays (except in the degenerate case when the geometry is allowed to contain cycles).

The intended **interpretation of a feature** is the set of time intervals in which the feature is present in the utterance. To express this, theories of phonological interpretation such as Bird and Klein 1990 map the representation of an oral consonant (4A), onto an event structure that can be described in simple set-theoretic notation as (5A), that of a prenasalized consonant like (4B) onto an event structure such as (5B), and that of a nasal consonant like (4C) onto an event structure such as (5C).

(4A)   (4B)   (4C)

```
    C               C               C
    |              / \              |
    O             N   O             N
```

(5A) $C \subset O$ (5B) $C \cap N \neq \emptyset \neq C \cap O, N < O$ (5C) $C \subset N$

Needless to say, the information contained in the event structure such as (5A) "as long as there is a consonant event, there is an oral event", or (5B) "a nasal and an oral event overlap with the consonant event, and

the nasal event precedes the oral event", is less than a full description
of the events taking place during the articulation of these segments[8].
Phonetically, the interval occupied by the consonant can be divided into
more homogeneous subintervals or microsegments such as *attack, hold,*
and *release* phases. Paolillo 1990 argues that such a three-fold distinction
is also justified on phonological grounds. At the boundaries of segments,
and even at the boundaries of the microsegments, we might find short
transition intervals that cannot be assigned to any (micro)segment without
some *ad hoc* criteria but (in keeping with the "strict" view of segments
discussed in sections 3.1 and 4.1 above) we will ignore this issue for
the moment. Most importantly, diagrammatic representations of these
events, such as (6) below[9],

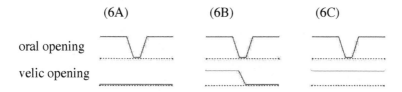

| (6A) | (6B) | (6C) |

oral opening

velic opening

need to be supplemented with precise timing information. Exactly when
does the consonant (or its phases) begin and end? When does the velum
begin to close, and when does the closure become complete? We will
specify this information, much like in the segmental case, in terms of
random variables. Ignoring the issues of transition phases for the moment,
and concentrating on the hold phase, we need one variable d_H to describe
the duration density of the hold interval, another variable d_N for the
(fully) nasal interval, and some means of describing the possibility of
synchronization (association line) between the two.

---

[8]Feinstein 1979 analyzes prenasalized stops bisegmentally (as nasal+stop clusters),
while Sagey 1986 takes them to be monosegmental. There are other representational
possibilities within autosegmental phonology; for example, Rosenthall 1988 argues for two
root nodes dominated by the same timing unit and sharing some class nodes. Here we will
treat prenasalized stops monosegmentally, as Fig. (4B) suggests. Our discussion owes a
great deal to Paolillo 1990, though it is not tied to the details of that proposal.
    [9]This figure is based on Fig. 4.1.1 of Paolillo 1990.

In order to incorporate the transition phases and/or transition microsegments, it is expedient to think of the interval occupied by a segment as a cycle and define various subintervals in terms of *phase angles* (Kelso and Tuller 1987). For example, if the attack phase occupies approximately the first 90 degrees, the hold phase approximately the following 180 degrees, and the release phase approximately the final 90 degrees of a full cycle, we can introduce four **phasepoint** variables taking values in the interval $[0, 2\pi]$: p_A for the the beginning of the attack, $q_A = p_H$ for the end of the attack (beginning of the hold), $q_H = p_R$ for the end of the hold (beginning of the release), and finally q_R for the end of the release. In the example, p_A and q_R are identically 0 and 2π respectively, so only $p_H \leq q_H$ are really interesting. These will describe when the hold phase begins and ends relative to the interval occupied by the whole segment.

The description of synchronization between two events on two tiers requires the specification of one phasepoint variable for each of the events, and possibly an additional random variable L for the description of the absolute time **lag** between the phasepoints. For example, in the prenasalization case depicted in (6B) above, the beginning of the consonant event precedes the raising of the velum by some time. This can be described by setting p_N and p_C to 0 (deterministically), and L to an appropriate random variable whose expected value is the average time delay. Alternatively, it can be described in relative terms, e.g. by saying that the 120 degree phase of the nasal event coincides (L=0) with the starting phase (0 degree) of the consonant event.

To give another example, in the *aspiration* of a voiceless consonant followed by a vowel, the tensing of the vocal folds (the 0 degree phase of the vowel event) will lag behind the stop release (which is, say, the 270 degree phase of the consonant event) by some time L. Again, alternative descriptions are possible. For instance, we can say that aspiration is internal to the consonant, being its 270 to 360 degree phase. This possibility of alternative descriptions suggests that in the description of synchronization we permit too many parameters. It is conceivable that

only the beginnings and ends of features can be synchronized in terms of
an absolute time lag, or that synchronization never involves a time lag,
just perfectly aligned phasepoints. The choice between these (or other)
possibilities should be determined experimentally.

A third, and perhaps more interesting, example is the "pundit's pronunciation" of Sanskrit vowels followed by *visarga*. This is described
by Coulson 1976 as producing the vowel, followed by the visarga (aspiration), followed by "a faint echo" of the vowel. Thus, in addition to
the duration density d_V of the vowel, we have to use the duration density
of the echo, say $.2d_V$, which will begin at the end of the aspiration. But
in order to describe that it is the *same* vowel that gets echoed, we must
assume that the shape of the oral cavity is preserved throughout the aspiration phase, suggesting an autosegmental analysis in which the unvoiced
event is defined as being in the middle of the voiced (vowel) event.

So far we have seen how a single binary feature is interpreted as a set
of intervals, and we have informally sketched the mechanism governing
the duration of such intervals and their synchronization, via phasepoints
and lags, to other features attached to the same node. Before describing
the synchronization mechanism more formally, let us first extend the notion of interval structures from binary to multivalued features. Formally,
an n-valued **interval system** is defined as an n-tuple of sets of (left closed,
right open) intervals such that

(7.1) No two intervals (in the same or in different sets) overlap,
(7.2) Every point of the real line belongs in exactly one interval,
(7.3) No interval is shorter than a positive constant MINDUR[10].

The idea is to view the ith member of the tuple as the collection of time
intervals in which the ith value of the feature is present in the utterance.
(It would be possible to use $n+1$-tuples for n-valued features, reserving

---

[10]For a discussion of the role of MINDUR see sections 3.1 and 3.3 above.

the 0th value for intervals of silence[11], but as we shall see in 4.3 below it is better to use a slightly more general concept and reserve the 0th value for those points where the feature is underspecified.) This is not to say that we intend to use multi-valued features as the basis of our semantic interpretation – on the contrary, we accept the position, carefully argued in McCarthy 1988, that the use of feature geometry makes multi-valued features largely unnecessary. Largely, but not (yet) totally – the evidence presented e.g. in Ladefoged 1971 that classically binary oppositions, such as *voiced* vs. *unvoiced,* reveal, upon closer inspection, rather finely graded phonetic scales, has not been fully assimilated in feature geometry. Thus we leave open the possibility of multi-valued features such as *high* vs. *mid* vs. *low tone*, but concentrate on the binary case below.

In order to model the use of class nodes dominating several (binary) features in the geometry we will have to extend the notion of (binary) interval systems to direct products of these. The resulting structures, when equipped with the appropriate synchronization, will be called *interval structures* and will form, recursively, the model structures we need to define the range of our interpretation function. Before turning this into a formal definition, let us present a few examples.

In the geometry proposed by McCarthy 1988 the root node contains the major class features [sonorant] and [consonantal]. This extends the original proposal of Clements and Keyser 1983 to distinguish C and V units in the direction suggested by Vágó 1984, who reserves a separate tier for major class information. From our perspective, the most important aspect of these proposals is that the "major class" tier receives its synchronization from the associated timing unit (or units, in the case of long segments) so that we do not expect the features on this tier to desynchronize. For such groups of features, the interval systems introduced above will provide an adequate representation, provided that we permit as many values as there are feature combinations.

---

[11]For our purposes it makes sense to treat silence as a full-blown segment occupying at least a single timing unit (cf. the silent demibeat of Selkirk 1984) or an integral number of timing units. We will return to this issue in section 5.3.

A different example is provided by the [coronal] node in McCarthy's proposal. Since its dependent features [distributed], [anterior], and [lateral] describe different aspects of tongue positioning, they are not expected to be fully synchronized with one another, a point that can be made even more clearly with respect to class nodes dominating features corresponding to different articulators the way [place] dominates both [labial] and [coronal] or the way the root dominates both [laryngeal] and [place]. In order to capture this lack of synchrony under [coronal], we need three separate (binary) interval systems for [distributed], [anterior], and [lateral]. To describe the total state of the [place] node, as it evolves in time, we need a simultaneous description of the three subordinated interval systems, complete with duration variables. The information content of the three simultaneous binary interval systems can be captured in a single octary system of intervals, called the **coarsest common refinement** (ccr) of the subordinated interval systems, and defined as follows:

(8.1) Every nonempty intersection in the form $I_1 \cap I_2 \cap \dots \cap I_k$, where the I_j are members of the jth subordinated interval system, will be a member of the ccr.

(8.2) The value of such an interval is the direct product of the values of the features obtaining in any timepoint of the interval.

It is trivial to verify that the ccr is well defined and meets criteria (7.1) and (7.2) of interval systems. However, it will not necessarily meet criterion (7.3) – it is quite conceivable that the lag between two intervals on different tiers is so small that in the coarsest common refinement an interval shorter than MINDUR is created. Were it not for this complication, we could use interval systems, as they stand, for model structures. As it is, we have to employ the more complex **interval structures** defined recursively as follows.

(9.1) Every n-valued interval system, equipped with a series of random duration density variables, one for each interval, is a type (n) interval structure.

(9.2) A type $(k_1, k_2, .., k_s)$ interval structure is the **freely aligned** direct product of type $(k_1), (k_2), .., (k_s)$ interval structures, which is equipped with s series of random duration variables (one series for each subordinate interval structure).

(9.3) A type $[(k_1, k_2, .., k_s), t]$ interval structure is the direct product of type $(k_1), (k_2), ..., (k_s)$ interval structures **aligned according to an interval system** t, equipped with $s + 1$ series of random phase variables (one series for the ccr of each subordinate interval structure and one for t) as well as with s series of random lag variables between the phasepoints of the subordinate structures and the phasepoints in t.

In general, interval structures are built from the basic components, given by (9.1), and from other interval structures, by means of free alignment (9.2), or alignment according to some interval system (9.3) recursively. Free alignment is used for class nodes such as [coronal] where the content of the class node is completely determined by the contents of the nodes dominated, so that no synchronization is expected, while alignment according to some interval system is used for class nodes such as [root] that have their own featural and temporal content to which synchronization of subordinate nodes can be anchored.

Aside from the phasepoint/lag mechanism, specifically designed to take care of the real time aspects of the representation, the construction of the model structures follows the construction of feature-geometrical trees very closely. This has the disadvantage that computations involving model structures are rather complex, but has the advantage of making the interpretation function simple, almost trivial. To see whether a tree dominated by a root note can be mapped on a given model structure, we need to check the tree against the structure recursively.

Again, rather than starting with the formal definition, first we give an informal (and considerably simplified) example. It is well known that nasal-obstruent clusters such as found in *rinse* or *hamster* often undergo a rule of *Intrusive Stop Formation* (ISF) to yield *nts, mps* on the surface. Anderson 1976 describes this in the following terms: "Since an oral sound is to follow the [m], the velum will have to be raised (...) and it is (...) plausible to imagine that the velum is raised earlier than necessary". Wetzels 1985 restates the main idea of this analysis in an autosegmental framework; the feature [–nasal] spreads leftward onto the preceding consonant which, as a result, turns into a prenasalized stop.

Abstracting away from all other features, in the underlying form [nasal] changes from + to – synchronously with the change in [continuant] from – to +. This is described by a simple interval structure in which the nasal and the continuant interval systems are aligned according to the timing tier, with no lag in either. IFS corresponds to a somewhat more complex interval structure in which a positive (say 30%) phase of the [–nasal] interval is aligned with the beginning of the second timing unit. This yields an intermediate [–continuant, –nasal] interval in the ccr which, when reanalyzed as a full segment, corresponds to the intrusive stop.

Clements (1987) argues that the proper way to view this phenomenon is *retarded* oral occlusion, rather than *advanced* velar opening. In this analysis, the [–continuant] spreads onto the following node, so that the domain of the intrusive stop is carved out from the domain of the obstruent following, rather than from the nasal preceding it. It is easy to see how this analysis can be rephrased in terms of interval structures. Again [continuant] and [nasal] are aligned according to the timing tier, but this time a positive (say 70%) phase of the [–continuant] is aligned with the end of the first timing unit.

The (local) **interpretation** of a segment (root node) can now be defined in a top-down recursive manner:

(10.1) If the root node contains features corresponding to the interval structure t and dominates class nodes of type $(k_1), (k_2), .., (k_s)$, the interpretation function maps it onto an interval structure of type $[(k_1, k_2, .., k_s), t]$.

(10.2) If a class node does not contain any features, and dominates (class) nodes of type $(k_1), (k_2), .., (k_s)$, the interpretation function maps it onto an interval structure of type $(k_1, k_2, .., k_s)$.

(10.3) A type (n) node is mapped onto an n-valued interval system.

Perhaps the most noteworthy feature of this definition is that it leaves the assignment of temporal structure free. This has the effect of leaving the interpretation of segments time-free, i.e. containing no more information than the original representation contained, namely information about the featural composition of the segment. This means, among other things, that when we compute the interpretation of adjacent [m] and [s], some of the interval structures that will fit this representation will also fit the representation [mps]. The whole range of model structures will of course distinguish between these two, but there will be structures that are models of both, which is the intended effect.

It is trivial to narrow down the above definition by requiring identically 0 phases and lags for subordinate tiers, and regular (say 80msec) intervals for timing units – this will yield the interpretation presented informally in 2.4.4. But this would have the undesirable side effect of creating, among other things, a strict distinction between [ms] and [mps]. Rather than insisting on some arbitrary phasepoint/lag structure, the formalization presented above gets exactly as much out of the interpretation as we put in the representation. In order to give more content to the interpretation, we will have to estimate the random variables that were left free here. As we shall see in chapter 5, this can be done by matching temporally fully specified interval structure tokens to interval structures with parameterized random variables.

4.3   The interpretation of large-scale structure

In the previous section we have discussed the interpretation of single
segments or a few adjacent segments. Here we turn to the large-scale
structural properties of speech, to phenomena that affect a large, in principle unbounded number of segments. Since it is well known that global
effects, such as the gradual declination of F_0 contours over larger domains, can be described as the cumulative result of local effects, such
as adjustment of pitch range across adjacent units (Liberman and Pierrehumbert 1984), the important distinction is not so much between smaller
and larger domains, as between *convex* and *non-convex* ones. In the
previous section we restricted our attention to intervals (convex temporal domains) – here we will investigate whether the use of non-convex
domains is also necessary for interpreting autosegmental representations.

Let us first briefly survey the range of phenomena that can be called
non-convex. Reduplication rules (see 2.2.4 and 2.5.3 above) often produce non-contiguous but otherwise homogeneous domains such as a repeated vowel, but such examples can always be reanalyzed as being composed of two independent domains, each by itself convex. Echo phenomena, such as the "pundit's pronunciation" discussed in 4.2 above, provide
better examples, but it is debatable whether they belong in (postlexical)
phonology proper. The most important phonological cases come under
the heading of *harmony systems*. Vowel harmony was illustrated in 2.2.3
above by the case of Hungarian[12], but harmony phenomena are in no way
restricted to vowels – we find a wide range of harmony systems affecting
consonants in various ways, ranging from nasal harmony (e.g. Guaraní,
see Poser 1982) to pharyngealization harmony (see Hoberman 1987).

Although in rare cases all segment types are affected by the harmony
process (so that the domain created ends up being convex), typically we

---

[12]We should note here that vowel harmony is by no means restricted to Hungarian or to
Uralic. Many major language families from Indo-European to Niger-Kordofanian contain
at least some languages with vowel harmony such as Montañes Spanish (see McCarthy
1984) or Akan (see Clements 1981).

find two classes of segments: *harmonizing* and *neutral.* While harmonizing segments share the same value for a feature or sets of features, neutral segments will not share at least one of the values. Since the harmonizing segments (typically, vowels) and the neutral segments (typically, consonants) appear interdigitated, harmony phenomena create a large variety of non-convex domains. In this section, I will first overview the commonly used strategies for dealing with such domains: in 4.3.1 *underspecification,* and in 4.3.2 the use of *hidden variables,* and argue that both of these involve a non-monotonic element. The interpretation function is then defined in 4.3.3 so as to accommodate both of these strategies.

4.3.1   Underspecification

Theories of underspecification come in several flavors (see Archangeli and Pulleyblank 1986, Steriade 1987) but the key idea is common to all varieties. In addition to segments taking positive and negative values for features, we also permit them to take no value at all – in such cases we call the segment **underspecified** for the feature in question. So far we have used such segments as archiphonemes, i.e. as a disjunction of the two fully specified segments that would be created by adding the positive or the negative feature value. But this concept, what we might call *two-sided underspecification,* does not really capture the way underspecified segments are actually used in phonology.

One important usage, called *trivial underspecification* in Steriade 1987, concerns the cases where a segment never acquires any value of the feature; Steriade's example is labial segments, which arguably never get specified for [anterior], since the tongue plays no role in the formation of labials. While this kind of justification for underspecification is not unappealing, from the perspective of the formalism developed in 4.1 above such cases must be viewed as cases of 3-valued features. To use Steriade's example, [anterior] divides the set of segments into three classes: those in which the tongue forms a constriction after the soft palate are [+anterior], those in which it forms a constriction at the soft palate are [–anterior], and those in which it plays no role are [0anterior]. Trivial underspecification might turn out to be a useful tool in phonology, but most practicing phonologists tend to avoid three-valued features and would reclassify the 0-valued segments as belonging to either the + or the – class.[13]

Another important usage, in fact the one I take to be central for all theories of underspecification, will be called *one-sided underspecification*. This means that the 0 feature value is treated as standing for only one value, a value that will be assigned by a later rule. In a typical harmony system, neutral segments will neither undergo nor block the spreading of either value of the harmonic feature – they are "transparent" in the sense that harmony works as if these segments were not present at all. Somewhat surprisingly, it is often the case that such neutral segments are, on the surface, specified for a definite value for the harmonic feature. Given the No Crossing Constraint of autosegmental phonology, we would expect such segments to block the spreading of the harmonic feature, but in a large class of cases they in fact do not block it. If we can maintain that at the point in the derivation where harmony applies, neutral segments are underspecified for the harmonizing feature, this transparent behavior makes sense. There is no association line to block the spreading and no floating feature to complicate it.

The intuitive picture behind this analysis is an extremely appealing one. The idea is that the domain *is* convex at the time when the harmony rule applies, and this convex domain gets broken up only at a later, possibly very late stage of the derivation. But there is a price to be paid for this idea – we are irrevocably committed to a procedural conception of the derivation, in which there can be earlier and later stages. To see that the commitment is in fact irrevocable, consider the harmonic spreading of the feature opposite to the surface specification of the neutral segments.

---

[13]In the case of [anterior], most phonologists would unhesitatingly put the labials in the [+anterior] class, since the dominant constriction, though not formed by the tongue, is obviously in the anterior region.

At the point where the harmony rule applies it spreads the wrong value on the neutral segments, for if it did not, the domain would not in fact be convex. Since the value at this stage is not what appears on the surface, there must be some later (default) rule that yields the correct surface value. This is, by definition, a feature changing (i.e. nonmonotonic) rule.

While the nonmonotonic element cannot be entirely eliminated, it can be pushed into the derivational morphology[14] by a judicious selection of one-sided and two-sided underspecification. As Vágó (1976) shows, the same morphemes (case markers) can serve as suffixes and as stems in Hungarian. If we treat the suffixes as containing archiphonemes (two-sided underspecification), their harmonizing behavior in the inflectional morphology can be explained, but the feature specifications with which these morphemes surface as stems must be deleted to get this effect. However, such nonmonotonic effects are widespread in derivational morphology at any rate, both in truncation (stray erasure) and in category-changing suffixation.

4.3.2   Hidden variables

The alternative approach, which I will call the *hidden variable* model, is based on an even more radical split between the surface value of a feature and the behavior of the segment. Rather than trying to bring the 0 (underspecified) value into play, it employs a separate feature, the hidden variable, to encode behavior that contradicts the surface specification. Harmonic spread does not affect each segment equally. The ones that get affected are distinguished from the ones that do not by the hidden variable. The idea here is that the domain is in fact not convex – rather, it is the harmonic *projection* (see 1.3 above) of the domain which is convex. The hidden variable or, in phonological parlance, *diacritically used feature*, comes into play because the projection process itself cannot be governed by the harmonic feature. There are segments, namely the neutral segments, which should not appear in the projection in spite of

---

[14]As pointed out by Kiparsky (pc), who attributes the idea to Harry van der Hulst.

the fact that they can carry the harmonic feature.

Here the intuitive picture is no less appealing. The idea is that the domain is not convex (i.e. not a contiguous substring) at any time in the derivation, but it *is* convex once a projection of the space is taken. Although the diacritic use of features has been rather forcefully condemned (see e.g. Kiparsky 1973), it still plays a crucial role in many analyses (for a recent example, see Hyman 1988). These contradictory tendencies can coexist only because it has not been widely recognized that the operation of taking a projection introduces abstractness, as there is material deleted by the projection. The operation of deleting diacritically used features is of course generally recognized to be a non-monotonic operation. This is not the place to sketch the historical developments that led from Kiparsky's (1973, originally 1968) Alternation Condition to the presently accepted view that seeks to explain cases of obligatory neutralization in terms of strict cyclic effects (see Kenstowicz and Kisseberth 1977, Ringen 1980, and in particular Kiparsky 1982). Suffice it to say that clear cases of obligatory neutralization, such as discussed in Vágó 1980 or Anderson 1981 remain, so that abstractness, though much better understood, is not entirely eliminated from phonological representations.

An important side-effect of autosegmentalization was that a large number of cases previously requiring diacritically used features are now analyzed in terms of floating features and other nonstandard configurations of features and association lines. To give an example, *h*-aspiré stems in French are now analyzed with an initial empty consonant slot (Clements and Keyser 1983, Goldsmith 1990) rather than with a diacritic [+*h*-aspiré]. Here again the advances in phonological theory led to a better understanding, but not to the elimination, of abstractness. The fact that different underlying representations can lead to the same surface form remains. Since in such cases information present in the underlying representation is destroyed in the course of the derivation, again we must conclude that phonology is non-monotonic.[15]

---

[15] A similar conclusion is reached, primarily on the basis of arguments concerning phonological change, in Bromberger and Halle 1989.

4.3.3 The interpretation function

The above considerations suggest that our view of phonetic interpretation needs to be refined in two important respects. First, condition (7.2) must be abandoned. Underspecification means that not every feature takes a definite value at all times. To capture this fact, n-valued interval systems must be replaced by $n + 1$-valued ones, in which the extra (0th) value corresponds to time periods for which the feature in question is underspecified[16]. Second, we must permit the interpretation function to be nonmonotonic to the extent that certain features (corresponding to the hidden variables) become "masked" in certain intervals. For example, the echo vowel following the visarga (see 4.2 above) is best understood by assuming that the oral features characterizing the preceding vowel are retained until after the echo, but are, in effect, masked during the aspiration. The same masking analysis is suggested by the Öhman 1967 model of vowel to vowel coarticulation (see also Keating 1988).

Therefore the global interpretation function is extended to contain a set of interval systems encoding hidden variables. The mapping between phonetic representations and the waveform will depend not only on the overt features but on the hidden ones as well. With this addition, global interpretation can be based on local interpretation the following way. Given an autosegmental representation A and an interval structure I, the (global) **interpretation** function maps A on I iff:

(11.1) For every root node in A, I has a part that is the interpretation of that node (segment) as defined in (10) above.

(11.2) Each non-zero valued interval for every overt feature in I is licensed by a segment in A or by a hidden feature, in an order-preserving manner.

(11.3) Contour features are mapped on adjacent level-valued intervals, with possibly 0-valued intervals in between.

---

[16]Whether a MINDUR condition on such intervals is reasonable remains to be seen.

These requirements capture the intuitive idea that the interpretation of a representation is the concatenation, possibly with 0-valued intervals in between, of the interpretations of the segment-size parts of the representation. (11.3) means that whenever a single unit, such as a vowel, is associated with a series of features on a single tier, such as a HLH melody, the interpretation is a set of intervals (in the example, H, L, and H) which can, but need not, be separated by shorter intervals on which the feature is underspecified. The dual situation, in which a single feature is spread over several segments, does not require a special provision, as it is handled by the same synchronization mechanism that was motivated by microsynchrony in 4.2 above.

With this last definition, the task of formalizing autosegmental phonology is completed. We inspected what phonologists do and explicated their practice in a more rigorous framework built from "logicomathematical" primitives. This framework enables us to turn autosegmental phonological descriptions of natural languages into rigorously defined, though not necessarily very effective, algorithms. Even more importantly, this framework will guide our efforts in chapter 5 to introduce a new, linguistically motivated architecture for Markov modeling of speech.

4.4 Appendix

In section 4.1 we motivated the use of features by their power to express natural classes and showed that feature geometry is a generalization of both the SPE and the Pāṇinian method of expressing such classes. But we did not motivate feature geometry itself (beyond the remark that a geometrical arrangement makes it possible to replace multi-valued features by class nodes), and we did not investigate its properties in any detail. The aim of this Appendix is to fill in this gap by showing what can, and, more importantly, what cannot be expressed by means of rooted labelnode trees.

The standard (rolodex) geometry contains no intermediate nodes between the root and the leaves of the tree. In order to justify the generality of the feature geometry scheme we need to demonstrate the utility of such *class* nodes. McCarthy 1988 lists three main reasons for using class nodes: processes of *assimilation*, processes of *reduction*, and *cooccurrence restrictions* corresponding to autosegmental association, delinking, and OCP effects, respectively. None of these phenomena can be stated on natural classes directly. Assimilation involves the natural correspondence of segments in two natural classes, reduction involves the relation between a natural class and a single segment, and cooccurrence restrictions involve the use of a well-formedness condition (Leben's Obligatory Contour Principle, see section 2.5.3) in a filtering manner (see section 2.2).

The overall effect of taking these phenomena into account is to define natural classes *of features* (see Clements 1987). Since we already have two methods, that of SPE, and that of Pāṇini, to deal with natural classes, the question must be asked: why do feature geometry? Why not define some metafeatures of features or anubandhas, or some metaśivasūtras of anubandhas or features? The answer provided below is that natural classes (both natural classes of features and natural classes of segments) have a particular kind of algebraic structure that makes feature geometry the appropriate tool to express natural classes. In 4.1 we have already seen some indications of the fact that natural classes of segments have some kind of algebraic structure. First we noted in proposition (2) that compared to the variety of classes that can be formed out of segments, only a vanishing fraction of classes are actually natural[17]. Second we noted in proposition (3) that the set N of natural classes is basically closed under intersection. If we are prepared to call singletons and the empty set natural, the qualifier "basically" can be dropped.

Thus we have reasons to believe that there is some algebraic structure to natural classes, and that this structure is almost, but not quite, boolean.

---

[17]The epistemological problem of why sparseness is an indicator of structure lies beyond the scope of this work.

N is closed under intersection, but not under complementation. Therefore it makes sense to look for some generalized boolean structure in natural classes and, as I will argue below, this is exactly what we find. First let us define, following Ehrenfeucht (pc), the notion of **independence**: two sets X and Y on some domain D are independent (denoted $X \nparallel Y$) iff none of the sets $X \setminus Y, Y \setminus X, X \cap Y, \overline{X \cup Y}$ are empty. Two sets X and Y are **semi-independent** (denoted $X \not\vdash Y$) iff none of the sets $X \setminus Y, Y \setminus X, X \cap Y$ are empty. Informally, independence means that no hierarchical inferences can be made. Knowing that some $p \in D$ is or is not a member of X gives us no information about its membership in Y.

Features (or classes of features) are not always (semi)independent. For instance if we know that a segment is [+low] we can infer that it is [−high]. But in the structures defined below, natural classes are not required to be (semi)independent of each other. The only requirement is that if two natural classes are (semi)independent then the sets formed from them must be also natural. Ehrenfeucht defines a set of sets $E \subset 2^D$ to be an **independent Boolean algebra** or IBA iff (i) $X, Y \in E, X \nparallel Y \Rightarrow X \cup Y, X \cap Y, X \setminus Y, Y \setminus X \in E$; (ii) $X \in E \Rightarrow \overline{X} \in E$; and (iii) $\emptyset, D, \{a\}, \overline{\{a\}} \in E$ (singleton sets and their complements). A set of sets $S \subset 2^D$ is a **semi-independent Boolean ring** or SIBR iff (i') $X, Y \in S, X \not\vdash Y \Rightarrow X \cup Y, X \cap Y, X \setminus Y, Y \setminus X \in S$; and (ii') $\emptyset, D, \{a\} \in S$ (singleton sets).

Can the set N of natural classes, perhaps suitably extended by the empty set and singletons, play the role of the set E in the above definitions? As we mentioned above, the complement of a natural class of segments need not be natural. For example, the complement of the set of mid vowels, being the set of high vowels plus low vowels plus consonants is anything but natural. Thus N is not an IBA. But it is a SIBR − if two natural classes of segments are neither contained in one another nor disjoint, their union, intersection, and differences will again be natural. The same can be said about natural classes of features, at least if we restrict our attention to classes established on the basis of assimilation evidence, for if a group of features X assimilates as a unit in some process p, and an overlapping group of features Y assimilates as a unit in some process q, and the two groups are not distinct, the segments that fit under both[18] will necessarily show both kinds of assimilation. If, on the other hand, the two sets of features are disjoint, the definition of SIBRs does not require that their union act in concert.

Before we make the argument that justifies feature geometry (as opposed to metafeatures or metaśivasūtras), let us consider a few simple examples of IBAs and SIBRs. First of all, the systems of sets listed in clause (iii) and (ii') of the above definition are obviously IBAs and SIBRs respectively – let us denote them by **A**. Second, traditional boolean algebras are of course IBAs and SIBRs – let us denote them by **B**. The third example (and the first nontrivial one) is the IBA built on GF(2,2), i.e. the 2-dimensional cube with points $a=(0,0)$, $b=(0,1)$, $c=(1,0)$, $d=(1,1)$, by including all subsets *except* $\{b,c\}$ and $\{a,d\}$. As the reader can easily verify, this 14-member set of sets is an IBA but not a SIBR. The key idea is to view these sets from the center of the square, so to speak, as segments in a cyclically ordered set of n points. If all such segments are included, we get an IBA, and if we break up the circle and use linear ordering, we get a SIBR. Let us denote the class of such interval structures by **C**.

The argument justifying feature geometry can now based on the fact that all IBAs and SIBRs can be built from the **A**,**B**, and **C** classes of IBAs and SIBRs introduced above by arranging these in a suitable tree structure. This fact, which is Ehrenfeucht's representation theorem of IBAs and SIBRs, means that any set of natural classes (of anything) can be described by repeated application of SPE-style feature analysis (**B**), Pāṇinian type sets of intervals[19] (**C**), and trivial sets (**A**) as long as it has

---

[18]There will always be such segments as long as the processes in question are self-dual, i.e. involve both the marked and the unmarked value of the feature.

[19]To see that such sets form SIBRs, consider two intervals $[AB]$ and $[CD]$. If they are semi-independent, their intersection is non-empty, so there is a segment x such that $x \leq B$ and $C \leq x$. Therefore, $C < B$ and by similar appeals to the nonemptiness of $[AB] \setminus [CD]$ and $[CD] \setminus [AB]$ it follows that $A \leq C \leq B \leq D$, and thus $[AC)$, $(BD]$, and $[AD]$ are

the closure properties described above. In other words, feature geometry is demonstrably sufficient for describing the structure of natural classes. But is it necessary? To show that it is, we have to find a set of classes that resists analysis in a purely feature-based or in a purely anubandha-based framework. Laryngeal features vs. place features vs. [continuant] vs. [nasal] (that is, the groups of features immediately dominated by [root] in McCarthy's analysis) provide exactly such an example. It is trivial to devise a system of metafeatures that would distinguish these four classes of features. But metafeatures would predict that some two-member combination of these four classes, such as [place]+[nasal] or [place]+[continuant] or [place]+[laryngeal] must itself be a natural class of features, and there is no evidence in favor of such a view. The same overgeneration argument can be made about metaśivasūtras. Thus we see that feature geometry is both necessary and sufficient – it is hard to imagine how phonological practice could receive stronger theoretical support.

Finally, we can gain a little more insight by comparing SIBRs to IBAs and by looking at the feature geometries that were proposed so far from the perspective of SIBRs. Ehrenfeucht's representation theorem implies that the only interesting class of IBAs that are not SIBRs will be the class of cyclic interval systems. Since such systems are outside the descriptive power of feature geometry, we should look at what it would take to find this situation in language. What is needed is a set of features that can be arranged in a cyclic order in such a manner that we find (assimilatory, reduction, or cooccurrence) evidence for the grouping of those features that form arcs of the cycle. Inspecting the set of features used in linguistics we cannot find such a cycle. Is this an accident? The theory tells us that it is not, because there is no reason to suppose that geometrically arranged feature sets are closed under complementation – the complement of a set of features dominated by a single class node is

---

also intervals. (The open intervals can be replaced by closed ones because there are only finitely many points involved.)

not expected to be dominated by some other class node.

Turning to the extant set of proposals (for a list of these, see section 1.5 above) we notice that the class **C** is absent from them. At the root node, all existing proposals have **A** structure, and at lower nodes, **A** or **B**. Here the lack of **C** structures cannot be explained by lack of closure under complementation, for Pāṇinian type sets of intervals are SIBRs which do not require such closure, and indeed we find a set of natural classes for which a Pāṇinian analysis is more appropriate than the SPE-type, namely the set of major classes. The relevant linear ordering is provided by the traditional sonority hierarchy (Grammont 1895, Jespersen 1904). If major classes are arranged in order of increasing sonority, we need only one anubandha (at the end) to express sonority-based generalizations such as the cross-linguistic variety of classes that can appear as syllabic nuclei. Within generative phonology, the first attempts to replace feature bundles by tree structures were motivated by the need to express the sonority hierarchy (Hankamer and Aissen 1974, Carlyle 1985). The present analysis suggests the theory of feature geometry has the resources to incorporate such analyses in a slightly modified fashion. Rather than encoding sonority by dominance in uniformly branching binary trees, it could be encoded by precedence in n-ary (flat) trees.

4.5 References

Anderson, Stephen R. 1976. Nasal consonants and the internal structure of the segments. *Language* **52** 326–344.

Anderson, Stephen R. 1981. Why phonology isn't "natural". *Linguistic Inquiry* **12** 493–540.

Archangeli, Diana 1985. Yokuts harmony: evidence for coplanar representation in nonlinear phonology. *Linguistic Inquiry* **16** 335–372.

Archangeli, Diana and D. Pulleyblank 1986. The content and structure of phonological representations, ms, U of Arizona.

Bird, Steven and Ewan H. Klein 1990. Phonological events. *Journal of Linguistics* **26** 33–56.

Bromberger, Sylvain and Morris Halle 1989. Why phonology is different. *Linguistic Inquiry* **20** 51–70.

Cardona, George 1965. On Pāṇini's morphophonemic principles. *Language* **41** 225–237.

Carlyle, Karen A. 1985. Sonority scales and the syllable template. *NELS* **15** 34–48.

Cherry, Colin 1956. Roman Jakobson's distinctive features as the normal coordinates of a language. In *For Roman Jakobson*, Morris Halle, (ed.) Mouton, The Hague.

Cherry, Colin 1957. *On human communication*. MIT Press, Cambridge.

Cherry, Colin, Morris Halle and Roman Jakobson 1953. Toward the logical description of languages in their phonemic aspect. *Language* **29** 34–46.

Clements, George N. 1981. Akan vowel harmony: a nonlinear analysis. In *Harvard Studies in Phonology*, George N. Clements, (ed.) vol. 2, IULC, 108–177.

Clements, George N. 1985. The geometry of phonological features. *Phonology Yearbook* **2** 225–252.

Clements, George N. 1987. Phonological feature representation and the description of intrusive stops. In *CLS Parasession on autosegmental and metrical phonology*, Anna Bosch, Barbara Need and Eric Schiller, (eds.) vol. 23, 29–50.

Clements, George N. and S. Jay Keyser 1983. *CV Phonology: A Generative Theory of the Syllable*. MIT Press, Cambridge.

Coulson, Michael 1976. *Sanskrit*. Teach Yourself Books, Hodder and Stoughton, Sevenoaks, Kent.

Ehrenfeucht, Andrzej pc. Personal communication.

4. Synchronization 163

Feinstein, Mark 1979. Prenasalization and syllable structure. *Linguistic Inquiry* **10** 245–278.

Goldsmith, John A. 1976. *Autosegmental Phonology*. PhD Thesis, MIT.

Goldsmith, John A. 1990. *Autosegmental and metrical phonology*. Basil Blackwell, Cambridge MA.

Grammont, M. 1895. La dissimilation consonantique dans les languages indo-européennes et dans les languages romanes, Dijon.

Halle, Morris 1964. On the bases of phonology. In *The structure of language*, Jerry A. Fodor and J. Katz, (eds.) Prentice-Hall, Englewood Cliffs, 324–333.

Hankamer, Jorge and Judith Aissen 1974. The sonority hierarchy. *CLS Parasession* **10** 131–145.

Hayes, Bruce 1986. Inalterability in CV phonology. *Language* **62** 321–351.

Hoberman, Robert D. 1987. Emphasis (pharyngealization) as an autosegmental harmony feature. In *CLS Parasession on autosegmental and metrical phonology*, Anna Bosch, Barbara Need and Eric Schiller, (eds.) vol. 23, 167–181.

Hulst, Harry van der 1988. The geometry of vocalic features, Leiden Papers in Linguistics and Phonetics.

Hulst, Harry van der and Norval Smith 1982. An overview of autosegmental and metrical phonology. In *The structure of phonological representations*, Harry van der Hulst and Norval Smith, (eds.) vol. 1, Foris, Dordrecht, 1–46.

Hyman, Larry M. 1988. Underspecification and vowel height transfer in Esimbi. *Phonology* **5** 255–273.

Jespersen, Otto 1904. *Lehrbuch der Phonetik*. B.G. Teubner, Leipzig.

Keating, Patricia A. 1988. Underspecification in phonetics. *Phonology* **5** 275–292.

Kelso, J.A.S. and B. Tuller 1987. Intrinsic time in speech production: theory, methodology, and preliminary observations. In *Motor and sensory processes of language*, Eric Keller and Myrna Gopnik, (eds.) Lawrence Erlbaum, Hillsdale NJ, 203–222.

Kenstowicz, Michael and Charles Kisseberth 1977. *Topics in Phonological Theory*. Academic Press, New York.

Kiparsky, Paul 1973. How abstract is phonology?. In *Three dimensions of linguistic theory*, Osamu Fujimura, (ed.) TEC, Tokyo, 5–56.

Kiparsky, Paul 1982. Lexical morphology and phonology. In *Linguistics in the morning calm*, I.-S. Yang, (ed.) Hanshin, Seoul, 3–91.

Kiparsky, Paul pc. Personal communication.

Ladefoged, Peter 1971. *Preliminaries to linguistic phonetics*. University of Chicago Press.

Liberman, Mark and Janet Pierrehumbert 1984. Intonational invariance under changes in pitch range and length. In *Language sound structure*, Mark Aronoff and Richard T. Oehrle, (eds.) MIT Press, Cambridge, 157–233.

McCarthy, John J. 1984. Theoretical consequences of Montanes vowel harmony. *Linguistic Inquiry* **15** 291–318.

McCarthy, John J. 1988. Feature geometry and dependency: a review. *Phonetica* **45** 84–108.

Öhman, Sven E. G. 1967. Numerical model of coarticulation. *JASA* **41** 310–320.

Paolillo, John C. 1990. Representing Sinhala prenasalised stops, ms, Stanford University.

Poser, William J. 1982. Phonological representation and action-at-a-distance. In *The structure of phonological representations*, Harry van der Hulst and Norval Smith, (eds.) vol. 2, Foris, Dordrecht, 121–158.

Ringen, Catherine O. 1980. A concrete analysis of Hungarian vowel harmony. In *Issues in Vowel Harmony*, Robert Vágó, (ed.) 135–154.

Rosenthall, Sam 1988. The representation of prenasalized consonants. In *WCCFL 7*, Hagit Borer, (ed.) CSLI, Stanford.

Sagey, Elizabeth 1986. *The representation of features and relations in non-linear phonology*. PhD Thesis, MIT.

Selkirk, Elisabeth O. 1984. *Phonology and Syntax: The Relation Between Sound and Structure*. MIT Press, Cambridge MA.

Staal, J. F 1962. A Method of Linguistic Description: the Order of Consonants According to Pāṇini. *Language* **38** 1–10.

Steriade, Donca 1987. Redundant values. In *CLS Parasession on Autosegmental and Metrical Phonology*, Anna Bosch, Barbara Need and Eric Schiller, (eds.) vol. 23, 339–362.

Vágó, Robert M. 1976. Theoretical implications of Hungarian vowel harmony. *Linguistic Inquiry* **7** 243–263.

Vágó, Robert M. 1980. *The Sound Pattern of Hungarian*. Georgetown University Press.

Vágó, Robert M. 1984. Degenerative CV level units, CUNY Queens College and Tel Aviv University, unpublished manuscript.

Wetzels, Leo W. 1985. The historical phonology of intrusive stops: a nonlinear description. *Canadian Journal of Linguistics* **30** 233–285.

Formal Phonology

Chapter 5

Structured Markov models

This work grew out of the conviction of the author that the performance of standard speech recognition systems, though still improving perceptibly, is approaching only a local optimum which is quite far from the actual performance requirements of large vocabulary, speaker independent, continuous speech recognition applications, and even farther from the ultimate goal of matching, and perhaps surpassing, human performance. In order to get beyond this local optimum, speech recognition needs some new concepts, and the most promising source of new conceptual machinery is phonological theory. Having studied the key concepts of autosegmental phonology in some depth in the preceding chapters, we are now in a position to recapitulate its basic insights in the framework of *structured* Markov models (sMMs).

It should be said at the outset that no sMM system has yet been built. The reader looking for a detailed description of a proven system with manifestly superior recognition performance will be disappointed by this chapter, where the emphasis is not so much on *how* sMMs work, but rather on *why* they should be built in the manner proposed here. Clearly, sMM systems have to go through the same process of gradual improvement as the standard HMM systems, and a great deal of engineering ingenuity will be required in this process before they approach their local optimum.

Since this could very well be a long way from the global optimum we all search for, instead of making exaggerated claims about the potential of sMMs, it is best to concentrate on the benefits that will of necessity accrue from the process of building different sMM systems.

Readers of the previous chapters will be acutely aware of the fact that autosegmental phonology, far from being a single theory generally accepted by the linguistic community, is a whole family of specific, often quite radically different proposals. This chapter presents a method for building different sMMs that faithfully reflect the structure of the different proposals. Comparison of the relative performance of such sMMs will therefore be valuable for the linguists who must choose between the different versions of autosegmental theory, even if in absolute terms recognition rate falls short of the demands posed by practical applications. There are, furthermore, some good reasons to believe that the performance of sMMs will in fact surpass that of standard HMM systems, and if this is so, the speech engineer will also find them to be a valuable tool.

The main reason why enhanced performance is expected is discussed in section 5.1, where the known problems of feature-based systems are enumerated. In section 5.2 we show how the standard concept of Markov models, in which a single model corresponds to a single segment (in some context), can be considered to be the model-theoretic interpretation of a segment-based theory of phonology. Since model-theoretic interpretation leads naturally to standard Markov models in the segmental case, it is expected to lead to something even better in the autosegmental case. This idea is explored in section 5.3, where the model-theoretic interpretation of autosegmental phonology developed in section 4.3 is used as a blueprint for sMMs, and the algorithm that leads to different sMMs for different versions of autosegmental theory is described. Whether sMMs avoid the problems listed at the beginning of 5.1 is discussed in the concluding section.

5.1 Features in Markov models

Let us first consider the problems which plague all feature-oriented research from Jakobson, Fant and Halle 1952 to Glass and Zue 1988. The major problem is that features lack well-understood acoustic cues. While certain features, such as voicing, are reasonably easy to detect, others, such as rounding, resist acoustic characterization. Even where acoustic cues can be found, it is rarely the case that a simple zero-one decision can be reached for every point in the signal. And where such a decision can in fact be made, the cut-points for different features tend not to coincide so segment boundaries cannot be established. Finally, even when the featural composition of a segment is known, the superposition of the acoustic cues corresponding to these features hardly ever yields the desirable signal. In other words, the context-dependency of segments is made much worse by the introduction of features, since the acoustic correlates of features depend not only on the preceding and following features, but on the simultaneous ones as well.

At first sight these problems seem to be insurmountable. But as the case of allophonic variation (Church 1983) shows, phenomena that are detrimental to the performance of one kind of system can sometimes, in a differently designed system, be actually exploited for performance enhancement. As I will argue here and in section 5.3 below, features provide a similar case. The main problem is not with the idea of characterizing segments by means of a decomposition into parallel units, but rather with the lack of synchronization among the features composing the bundle. Ideally, we would have a sequence of cut-points demarcating segments in a neat concatenative fashion, as shown in (1) below:

(1)

t	a	m

If all features are perfectly synchronized, we have an SPE-type decomposition into features:

(2)

+cons	-cons	+cons
-voi	+voi	+voi
-nas	-nas	+nas
:	:	:

As is well known from articulatory studies such as Fujimura 1981, in practice we often fail to find synchronous cut-points. The kind of situation shown in (3) below (where voice onset is slightly delayed, and the end of the vowel is nasalized) is much more typical than the idealized situation depicted in (1) or (2).

(3)

+cons	-cons	+cons
-voi	+voi	
-nas		+nas
:	:	:

As we discussed at the end of section 4.1 above, it is possible to interpret this situation as a sign of the inherent fuzziness of the notion "segment". Whether we commit ourselves to the view that segment boundaries are fuzzy is immaterial – the lack of perfect synchrony (known in autosegmental phonology as the "failure of the Absolute Slicing Hypothesis", see Goldsmith 1976) is real, and poses serious problems for the standard Markov systems, which are built from segment (triphone) models.

One might object that the longer the units used by the system, the fewer boundaries there are, so the problem is not as serious as it seems[1]. But this objection, though not unreasonable in the light of the fact that many current systems indeed employ demisyllable-, syllable-, word-sized

---

[1] While in suprasegmental phonology the idea of 'precompiled' units recently gained some currency (Hayes 1990), in segmental phonology the possibility of precompiled units is rarely admitted. The experience with speech recognition and synthesis systems, however, points to the conclusion that such units must be recognized e.g. for function words.

or even longer units, is missing the point. The longer the basic unit, the harder it becomes to share training data across units. In particular, systems based on word-sized units, in which the fuzzy segment boundary problem is reduced to the problem of fuzzy word boundaries (in connected speech), can at best share data across the same words appearing in different compounds and affixed forms.

A large-vocabulary system, as this term is currently understood, will have between 10,000 and 200,000 lexical entries, typically around 50,000. But experience with large corpora shows that a 10,000 word vocabulary will cover only about 95% of tokens[2], a figure quite comparable to the recognition rate of medium-size (1,000 to 10,000 words) systems. For example, Jelinek, Mercer and Roukos 1990 report that adding the newly encountered words to the 20,000 lexical entries in the Tangora isolated word speech recognition system reduces the error rate from 2-3% to 1%. But the new word types are of course less frequent than the ones already added, so training data for them will be sparse. This is a serious problem for a lexicon based on longer units, but if the lexicon is based on smaller units (such as triphones) new entries can be added without altering the underlying models, i.e. even in the complete absence of training data.

Thus the overall performance of large vocabulary systems is determined on the margin. A hypothetical fivefold decrease in error rate[3] on the known vocabulary of say 50,000 words would only bring a 20% decrease in the overall error rate. 80% of the performance gain will therefore come from improving the performance of the productive part, i.e. the segment models. Since we cannot circumvent the problem of fuzzy boundaries by using longer units (because this would make it harder to share training data, already scarce, across the models), a new design which exploits the patterns of desynchronization should be of some interest to speech engineers. Because the sMM framework presented in section 5.3 is a

---

[2]For the statistical reasons behind this phenomenon, see Good 1953.

[3]It took the entire 15-year history of Hidden Markov Models to create one such decrease, and there is no reason to believe that the next one will happen any faster.

faithful model of autosegmental phonology, where the fuzziness of segment boundaries, "the failure of Absolute Slicing" is built into the theory,
we have good reason to expect improved performance on the margin,
where it really matters.

There is another, independent reason to believe that sMMs might do
well. Autosegmental phonology rests not only on the kind of *subsegmental* evidence discussed above, but also on a great deal of *suprasegmental*
evidence coming from the large-scale structure of speech (see section 4.3
above). Since autosegmental phonology deals with large-scale structure
quite successfully, sMMs are also expected to be successful to the extent
that they replicate autosegmentalization. The formalization of autosegmental phonology developed in the previous chapters covers large-scale
structure from unbounded spreading (see section 1.3) to templatic effects
(see section 2.2), and in the light of our discussion of hidden variables
(see section 4.3), sMMs have the resources to cover the same phenomena. However, the treatment of large-scale structure in sMMs will not be
given a prominent role in what follows, because such structure is most
clearly manifested in root and pattern morphology, vowel harmony, and
other phenomena not found in English[4].

5.2   The segment-based model

In this section we investigate the relation of the typical segment-based
and feature-based models from the perspective of our model-theoretic
formalization of phonology. While this perspective is useful inasmuch
as it leads to the proportion "standard (SPE) phonology is to standard
(left-to-right) HMMs as autosegmental phonology is to sMMs", in what
follows the language of model-theoretic semantics is largely abandoned
in favor of the language of statistics which is expected to be more familiar

---

[4]In speech engineering, where 90% of the work deals with English, there is a strong
tendency to ignore large-scale structure entirely. It is probably no accident that the only
domain where autosegmental phonology had a significant impact on speech engineering is
intonation (Pierrehumbert 1980,Pierrehumbert 1981), the only domain in English for which
large-scale structure is evidently important.

to the speech engineer[5]. Our starting point will be the segment-based interpretation defined in section 3.5, which maps autosegmental representations onto strings of left-to-right Markov models so that a separate Markov model corresponds to each segment (root node) in the representation. While in chapter 3 this interpretation was introduced only in order to describe the duration of the segments in the representation, the mechanism of course extends to the content of the segments. In what follows spectral parameters, amplitude, and possibly low order derivatives of these will all be lumped together as **content**. This is not to deny the practical importance of the mode of signal processing chosen, but rather to emphasize that our considerations are independent of the details of the signal processing "front end".

Like the duration, the content of a single segment token is deterministically given as a sequence of parameter vectors produced by the front end. And like the duration, **the content of a phonological representation** is defined as the statistical ensemble of the deterministic values for those tokens that fit the representation. Duration, as an ensemble, can be expressed in a single random variable, but content requires a more sophisticated data structure. While duration requires only a single real parameter, content must be viewed as an n-dimensional vector of real numbers[6], and this complicates the data structure to some extent. A more serious complication, not amenable to a vector quantization solution, is that the number of parameter vectors in the content sequence is itself random, being determined by the duration.

As is well known, HMMs provide an effective method for generating random length sequences of parameter vectors. On any run, the model will go through a sequence of states and emit, in each state, a vector according to the output distribution characterizing the state in question. But there are other possibilities, for example defining shorter (longer)

---

[5]In particular, the term 'model' will be used to abbreviate 'Markov model'. In the few cases where the model-theoretic meaning is intended, the more explicit phrase 'model structure' will be used.

[6]Except for discrete density systems.

sequences of vectors by downsampling (upsampling) a fixed-length template (Ostendorf and Ruocos 1989), so choosing Markov models for the purpose of capturing the content of phonological representations has to be justified by showing that the statistical structure embodied in Markov models is flexible enough to model the actual distribution of content. As far as the length of the sequences is concerned, in section 3.5 we already demonstrated that the statistical structure of *input* models is flexible enough to model any distribution that might arise. But as we shall see shortly, no similar "completeness" result can be established for content, not even for the simplest case of sequences of length one.

The problem, hardly ever discussed in the speech engineering literature, is that there is no guarantee that Markov models will continually improve as the population of phones becomes more and more narrowly circumscribed. Intuitively it seems obvious that dividing the population of, say, b phones into word-initial, word-internal, and word-final b-s and training separately for the three classes will improve the overall fit (as long as we have enough training data for each of the resulting classes), since we have three times more parameters to fit. But in fact this need not be true at all, as the following simple construction shows. Let us suppose that we use gaussians in the output and we model the following ensemble of sequences of length one: $p(0) = p(5) = 1/32; p(1) = p(4) = 5/32;$ $p(2) = p(3) = 10/32$. Since this is a binomial distribution, we can fit a very close gaussian. Now if we divide the population to three parts, the first being $\{0,5\}$, the second being $\{1,3\}$, and the third being $\{2,4\}$ (keeping the probabilities as they were), all three will have bimodal distributions so the gaussian approximation will be so bad that the overall error is in fact increased[7].

In this example, the result of dividing the population into more narrowly circumscribed groups and modeling each turns out to be worse than the result of using just one broad model. It is tempting to object to

---

[7]Similar examples can be created for all major families of distributions that one might consider, instead of gaussians, for output. Only discrete density systems that use full histograms instead of parametrized distributions in the output are immune to this problem.

the contrived nature of the example, but of course there is no guarantee that the actual subdivision process, which is usually carried out on the basis of expert knowledge about relevant contexts, will fare any better[8]. In fact, as we turn to more realistic examples that involve sequences of content vectors of different length, vectors corresponding to different phases of the training tokens will be, to a certain extent, averaged together. Because of this, it is by no means obvious that the distribution of sequences of vectors generated by Markov models will successfully approximate the characteristics of the population distribution. The fact that significant improvements can be realized from dividing segments into successive microsegments (see Deng, Lennig and Mermelstein 1990) indicates that the segment-based markovian scheme is actually vulnerable to this "warp-averaging" effect. In contrast, the feature-based system introduced in 5.3 is immune to this problem for the majority of features, namely the ones that do not form contours.

In spite of such theoretical misgivings, Markov models work quite well in practice. Though linguists generally ignore finite automata ever since Chomsky 1957 demonstrated the inadequacy of deterministic finite automata for syntax, and Miller and Chomsky 1963 made the point that probabilistic finite automata do not scale up (again for syntax), the performance of state of the art speech recognition systems like Sphinx (Lee et al. 1990b), syntactic taggers (Church 1988), and even machine translation systems (Brown et al. 1990) is good enough to make one believe that finite automata, much like context-free grammars in syntax, were dismissed too rashly. In particular, the markovian interpretation of segments, which is the conceptual model implicit in most working speech recognition systems, should be contrasted with the model of speech recognition inspired by the traditional organization of generative phonology:

---

[8]Even under approaches that strive to eliminate expert knowledge as in Lee et al. 1990a or Bahl et al. 1991, the best that can be guaranteed is that no division that would make matters worse (as in the above example) will be actually performed. But there is no guarantee that the population distributions can be approximated with arbitrary precision.

(4)

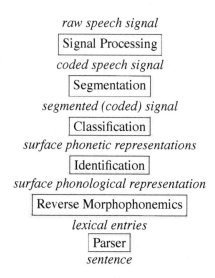

raw speech signal

Signal Processing

coded speech signal

Segmentation

segmented (coded) signal

Classification

surface phonetic representations

Identification

surface phonological representation

Reverse Morphophonemics

lexical entries

Parser

sentence

In what follows, I will call this model, exemplified by such systems as HWIM (Woods et al. 1976), the Segmentation – Classification – Identification or S-C-I model. Compared to (4), the model used by the majority of speech engineers is strikingly simple:

(5)

raw speech signal

Signal Processing

coded speech signal

Hidden Markov Model

sentence

The simplicity of this model is very strongly motivated by the difficulties with creating explicit Segmentation, Classification, and Identification algorithms. As Makhoul and Schwartz (1986) emphasize, linguists do not have a sufficiently detailed knowledge of context effects and the micro-synchrony of features to create good algorithms, while statistical models can be optimized to capture regularities in the data by general-purpose algorithms (e.g. Baum et al. 1970) that do not require such detailed advance knowledge about the domain.

In the S-C-I model decisions must be made at each stage, and errors introduced at some early stage have a devastating effect on the performance of later stages. In contrast, standard HMM systems combine the structural representations of segments (triphones), the structural representations of words (built from triphones or from larger units), and the structural representation of sentences (finite state parses) into a single language model on which optimization and search can be performed globally. This way decisions can be delayed until the moment of lexical choice or, if a finite state syntax is used, even further. Thus one is led to the conclusion that if feature-based systems are to be competitive with the segment-based systems dominating the field of speech recognition, they must be both trainable and able to make delayed decisions.

5.3   The feature-based model

For a book that promotes the use of phonological features in speech recognition it is something of an embarrassment to admit that there is no generally agreed upon version of feature theory to promote. Unfortunately, there is no firm consensus among phonologists about the number of features present in the universal system of features, about the precise nature of these features (are they all binary?), about the feature analysis of particular phonemes in particular languages, or about the geometry (see section 4.1 above) in which the features are arranged[9]. This is one of the areas where the abstract method of the work (see section 0.3) has real advantages. Given an arbitrary inventory of features arranged in an arbitrary geometry, we can construct a structured Markov model reflecting the inventory and the geometry in every detail by a simple recursive procedure traversing the tree that encodes the geometry in a

---

[9]The reader interested in the actual range of opinions about these matters should compare the papers collected in Itô et al. 1991 with one another.

bottom up fashion. This way we can evaluate different hypotheses about feature inventories and geometries on the basis of the performance of the corresponding sMMs.

In order to present the crucial steps of this construction, we will draw on our understanding of autosegmental phonology, as summarized in the concepts of model structures and model-theoretic interpretation developed in the previous chapter. In 5.3.1 we describe the markovian analog of interval structures (see section 4.2), which are small ergodic models called *feature models* – these are the basic building blocks of sMMs. In 5.3.2 we take the two basic modes of combining smaller interval structures into larger ones, free alignment and alignment according to an interval structure (see section 4.2), and describe the markovian analog of these constructions called *direct product* and *cascading*. The class of sMMs obtained from the feature models by recursive application of the direct product and the cascading constructions is somewhat similar to the class of Multi-Layer Perceptrons (MLPs). The relationship between the two is the subject of 5.3.3. The procedure of translating different versions of feature geometry into sMMs is explained in 5.3.4 using Clements' (1985) original proposal. Finally in 5.3.5 we reverse the direction of the translation and show how knowledge about the acoustic domain can be expressed in feature geometrical terms.

5.3.1   Feature models

The basic building block of our model structures for autosegmental phonology was the interval system (see section 4.2 above). Here an n-valued interval system will be replaced by a Markov model with n (hidden) states. These **feature models** are in state i whenever the feature has the ith value, somewhat like in *acoustic/phonetic decoder* of Levinson et al. 1989. Here the basic model has one state per feature value, rather than one state per phoneme, but there is a conceptual similarity inasmuch as the hidden states correspond to linguistically meaningful concepts, and there is considerable formal similarity inasmuch as both models are ergodic (as opposed to the standard left-to-right assumption, see section 3.4 above). An important difference between the basic feature model and the acoustic/phonetic decoder is that in feature models the duration is not controlled explicitly. Given that features tend to persist for intervals longer than the duration of a single segment, the transition probabilities are set so as to encourage the feature model staying in one state, i.e. high in the diagonal of the transition matrix and low everywhere else[10]. Naturally, a single feature model will not be sufficient to determine the identity of segments (or larger units) – for this we will need several feature models, trained on different features, to run in parallel.

The training of feature models requires pre-segmented and labeled data. If we have a corpus of pre-segmented, labeled utterances, we can simply divide the segments into as many groups as there are feature values, and use the averaged contents of each group as an estimate of the output distribution of the corresponding state. For example, if the feature model to be trained is [coronal], there will be one group of segments that are linguistically classified as [+coronal], and these are used to estimate the output distribution of the + state of the model, and similarly for the – state. Those segments which are predicted by phonology to be underspecified for [coronal] are used to estimate the output distribution for the 0th state. In practice, task-specific algorithms such as the *competitive training* proposed by Young (1990) are expected to be much more effective than the crude training method proposed above. Here and below the point is not so much to advocate the use of averaging algorithms over more task-specific algorithms, as it is to demonstrate the theoretical possibility of devising training algorithms for models incorporating features.

---

[10]If we interpret, as suggested in section 4.3 above, the 0th state as the state where no feature value can be reliably established, transition probabilities into this state should be set low and out of it high so as to encourage the model to make decisions.

5.3.2   Building structured models

The model structures for autosegmental phonology, interval structures, were built in chapter 4 from interval systems by means of two constructions called *freely aligned* and *aligned according to an interval structure* – let us take each in turn. Markov models, being finite automata, lend themselves naturally to a direct product construction. If the multiplicands have state sets $T_1, ..., T_k$, the product model will have states in the cartesian product of the sets $T_1 \times ... \times T_k$. The transition probabilities of the product model are given by the product of the transition probabilities in the components, and the output distribution of a product state will be the mixture of the outputs of the component states. Since the output distributions for any feature model are expected to cover almost the whole space, the mixtures, in the case of full covariance gaussians, are expected to look much like the intersections of the high probability regions of the component distributions.

The idea of direct product decomposition has been successfully applied in the Markov modeling of speech contaminated with noise (Varga and Moore 1990). The direct product construction is quite suitable for this case, as there is no reason to believe that the speech and the noise are in any way synchronized. In the case of features, however, we expect a great deal of synchronization. For instance, whenever voicing begins or ends, at least one major category feature is likely to shift since clusters of segments sharing the same major category tend to assimilate to one member (usually the first or the last, depending on the language) of the cluster in voicing. Thus we need a markovian version of alignment according to an interval structure. We will call this **cascading.**

In order to present the key idea of cascading, it will be convenient to think of Markov models as transducers that produce, for any sequence of parameter vectors, an optimal sequence of states (which can be computed by the Viterbi algorithm). If we have n Markov models, $HMM_1, HMM_2, ...HMM_n$ corresponding to the n interval structures which we wish to make the direct product of, plus a model HMM_0 corresponding to the interval system governing the alignment, arrange these in a two level scheme as follows:

(6)

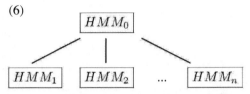

In the cascade arrangement, the models HMM_1, HMM_2, ... HMM_n on the lower level run in parallel. They are presented with the same parameter vectors frame by frame. Their maximum likelihood states, taken jointly, form a new "metaparameter" vector for each frame, and the output distributions of the top level machine HMM_0 will be estimated (by some version of the Baum-Welch algorithm, see e.g. Dempster, Laird and Rubin 1977) so as to maximize the likelihood of these metaparameter sequences. Although the top-level models could be word models or even larger, the linguistic theory behind this scheme is more faithfully replicated by taking these models to be *class nodes* (see sections 1.5 and 4.2). The aim of alignment, as defined by (9.3) in section 4.2, was to control (synchronize) the temporal behavior of the lower level models according to some interval system (the top level model).

Association lines are synchronization signals that enforce temporal overlap between two intervals (features) contained in different interval systems (tiers). In a markovian framework this means that certain states in the lower machines, namely those that correspond to the associated feature values, will appear with joint probability 1 in the output distribution associated with the state corresponding to the segment that shows the association[11]. The full range of interval structures thus can be embodied in a markovian framework by using the direct product and the cascade

---

[11]The phasepoint/lag mechanism described in section 4.2 will thus come into play only to the extent that increased phonetic knowledge makes it possible to replace markovian feature, class, and segment models by semi-markov models in the sense of Russell and Moore 1985. How such knowledge can be gained using sMMs is discussed in 5.3.5 below.

constructions recursively, so the class of **structured Markov Models** (sMMs) is defined as the smallest set which includes feature models and is closed under direct product and cascading[12].

5.3.3   Structured Markov Models and Multi-Layer Perceptrons

Before turning to examples of more complex feature geometries, let us first compare the simplest arrangement given in (6), which corresponds to the "rolodex" geometry of features discussed in section 4.1 above, to the model recently investigated in Meng and Zue 1991. The HMMs at the bottom level can be thought of as feature detectors, and the HMM at the top acts as a segment recognizer. Thus the main difference from the Meng and Zue model is the consistent application of the Markov paradigm. Meng and Zue use expertise-based feature detectors at the lower level and a neural net classifier at the top level, while here we see HMMs at both levels. The theoretical advantage stemming from using trainable models for features was discussed above – in practice it remains to be seen whether trained feature detectors will actually provide better results than expertise based detectors of the kind used in the FEATURE system developed at CMU (Cole et al. 1983, Cole et al. 1986).

At the top level, using an HMM, rather than a neural classifier, is also expected to be beneficial inasmuch as (semi)Markov models have a clear temporal structure absent from the kind of (non-recurrent) neural nets employed by Meng and Zue. Autosegmental phonology was developed because of the failure of the Absolute Slicing Hypothesis – features do not change their values simultaneously. Although phonologists or phoneticians do not have a full understanding of the way the changes in

---

[12]While the class of sMMs so defined is infinite, both the branching factor (number of features dominated by a class node), the depth (length of chains of class nodes), and the breadth (number of leaves) can be rather sharply delimited on the basis of the feature geometry trees proposed so far. Since sMM training is roughly the same order of complexity as standard HMM training, it is tempting to speculate that with improved hardware an exhaustive search could be performed on the class delimited by a branching factor <10, depth <5, and breadth <25.

one feature lag behind the changes in another one, at this point they are very much aware of the fact that such time lags are the rule rather than the exception. Thus we expect that a great deal of regularity is present in the patterns in the time lags, i.e. that the dynamics of the feature configuration will aid the recognition.

Is this arrangement very different from a two-layer perceptron, and, in general, are the more complex recursive structures to be discussed below very different from Multi-Layer Perceptrons (MLPs)? From a broad theoretical perspective they are not very different, because every Markov model can be implemented as a recurrent neural network (see Bridle 1990). The similarity between sMMs and MLPs can in fact be increased by taking the probability scores of the lower level HMMs being in the various states, rather than the index of the maximum likelihood states, as parameter vectors for the HMM on the top level. By doing this, we get classifiers producing continuous scores, rather than discrete on/off input units, at the first layer that provides the input for the hidden units (class nodes) in later layers.

In a more narrow practical sense, however, there are considerable differences between MLPs and sMMs. The primary difference is that MLPs are trained with hill-climbing methods which, at the present state of computing hardware, do not scale up from very small vocabulary (typically digit recognition tasks) to the large vocabularies required for more demanding applications. In contrast sMMs are trained in two passes[13]. The first pass is bootstrapped on standard HMM-based segmentation, and only the second pass uses hill-climbing, which reduces the problem to manageable proportions. A conceptually secondary, but for applications nonetheless very important difference is that the generic architecture of MLPs is replaced in sMMs by a task-specific architecture dictated by phonological theory.

---

[13]In the general case to be discussed below, the number of passes is determined by the depth of the feature geometry tree.

5.3.4   Expressing feature geometry in structured Markov models

Let us now turn to the procedure that translates various proposals about feature geometry to the corresponding structured Markov model. Since the input to this procedure is to be found in scholarly papers rather than in the mathematical objects (trees) that were used in section 4.1 and 4.4 for the formal analysis of feature geometry, we will present the translation procedure using the original proposal of Clements (1985), shown in (7) below, as our example.

(7)

rt = root	sl = supralaryngeal	l = laryngeal
m = manner	p = place	
sg = spread glottis	cg = constricted glottis	voi = voice
n = nasal	cn = continuant	st = strident
co = coronal	an = anterior	di = distributed

At first sight, we need nine[14] feature models at the lowest level, three corresponding to manner features, three to place features, and three to laryngeal features. In fact, we will need only six: three for manner, one for place, and two for laryngeal features. As the example of Intrusive Stop Formation discussed in section 4.2 shows, manner features are indeed capable of desynchronization, so in order to describe these we need three independent HMMs, namely HMM_n, HMM_{cn}, and HMM_{st},

---

[14]It is obvious from Clements' discussion that there are other features, e.g. vowel features or those describing tonal distinctions, that should be added to the geometry at the appropriate places. I will follow Clements in ignoring these.

aligned according to a fourth one, namely HMM_m (see figure (8A) below). However, the place features do not obviously show the same desynchronization effect, so we describe the whole subtree rooted in the place node with a single (8-valued) HMM_p. In languages where fewer place contrasts are present the model will have fewer states (see figure (8B) below). Finally, the subtree rooted in the laryngeal class node will of necessity give rise to fewer than 8 combinations, since [+sg] and [+cg] cannot cooccur. To simplify the discussion here and in what follows, I will assume that the remaining 3 values are sufficient for describing glottal stricture. Under this assumption, we can model the laryngeal subtree by the direct product of a 3-valued model, corresponding to the 3 combinations permitted by [sg] and [cg] together, and a 2-valued model, corresponding to the voiced/unvoiced distinction (see figure (8C) below).

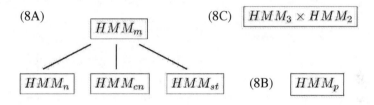

(8A)

$$HMM_m$$

$$HMM_n \quad HMM_{cn} \quad HMM_{st}$$

(8C) $$\boxed{HMM_3 \times HMM_2}$$

(8B) $$\boxed{HMM_p}$$

In the type notation introduced in section 4.2, (8A) is given by [(2,2,2),m], (8B) by (p), and (8C) by (3,2) if no 0th states are employed – m is the number of possible manners of articulation, and p is the number of possible places of articulation. If we use 0th states, (8A) is of type [(3,3,3),m+1], (8B) is of type (p+1), and (8C) is of type (4,3). Thus at the lowest level all three major types of interval structures (as summarized in (9) of section 4.2 above) are attested. Manner gives rise to direct product aligned according to an interval system as in (8A), place gives rise to a multi-valued interval system as in (8B), and laryngeal gives rise to freely aligned direct product as in (8C). In particular, the distinction between multi-valued interval systems, in which every interval is subject to a MINDUR restriction, and freely aligned direct product, where no such restriction is present, is exemplified by place vs. laryngeal. In the ccr (coarsest common refinement, see section 4.2) of place features every interval corresponds to a place description of some segment, so MINDUR is the overall segmental MINDUR which is about 20 milliseconds[15]. But in the ccr of laryngeal features the lack of synchrony between the spreading/constriction of the glottis and the onset or offset of voicing can lead to arbitrarily small intervals (cf. Fig. 6 in Ladefoged 1971), which can only be captured by the freely aligned direct product construction.

Let us denote the three sMMs constructed so far by sMM_m (8A), sMM_p (8B), and sMM_l (8C). Of these, the place model sMM_p and the laryngeal model sMM_l are ordinary HMMs. sMM_p is a p(+1) state ergodic model, and sMM_l, though the direct product of smaller HMMs, is still a standard HMM that will, in any single move, output a parameter vector according to the output distribution of its present state, and move into a new state according to the transition probabilities from its present state. But the operation of sMM_m is more complex. In a single move (corresponding to a single frame) all three lower level HMMs in it will move to a new (possibly the same) state and the record of these moves constitutes a "metaparameter" vector which plays the same role in the output distributions of the top level HMM of sMM_m (namely HMM_m) as the ordinary parameter vectors, derived from the speech signal, play in the output distributions of the lower level HMMs – they make up the statistical ensembles captured in the model. For example, if the manners of articulation permitted in the language are stop, fricative, approximant (including vowels), and trill, HMM_m will have four ergodic states (ignoring the 0th state), and will have to move into one of these based on the transition pattern of the lower HMMs (that is, without the benefit of direct information about the signal).

Thus, at the lowest level we have the three sMMs shown in (8) above. At the next level the manner model sMM_m and the place model sMM_p are put together into the supralaryngeal model sMM_{sl}, and at the highest (third) level the laryngeal model sMM_l is put together with the

---

[15] See fn. 5 to section 3.1.

supralaryngeal model to form the root model sMM_r which is a phone
(or phone in context) model. Since manner and place are completely
independent, we use the freely aligned direct product construction to
create an mp state supralaryngeal model $sMM_{sl} = sMM_m \times sMM_p$
for each archiphoneme *modulo* laryngeal distinctions (see section 4.2, and
the discussion of *sāvarṇya* in section 4.1 above). But the laryngeal and
supralaryngeal class nodes are not completely independent (the freeness
of voice onset is already handled by the laryngeal class node) so at the
top (root) level we again use cascading (alignment according to timing
units). The result is shown in (9) below:

(9)

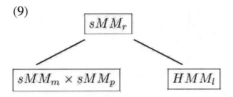

As can be seen from (9), the root (phone) models structured according
to Clements' geometry receive information from the signal most directly
through the laryngeal sub-sMM. In other words, the system is really
driven by voicing decisions, which can change the state of the laryngeal
model directly, while place and manner decisions are both based on the
joint effects of lower feature models.

While the example makes clear that translating proposals about feature geometry into sMMs is not entirely mechanical, it only requires
expert knowledge about the various proposals to the extent that the MIN-
DUR condition and the possibility of desynchronization at each class
node has to be ascertained by the translator, since this will determine the
choice between direct product, cascading, and (at the lowest level) multivalued features. If proposals about feature geometry came annotated
with this information, the procedure would be quite mechanical.

5.3.5 Acoustic feature geometry

In phonology, feature geometry is used to express knowledge about the inventory of cooccurrence restrictions and assimilation and reduction processes to be found in the languages of the world. It would not be totally surprising if a theory based entirely on this kind of purely grammatical evidence would fail to make realistic predictions about the acoustic phonetic aspect of speech. After all, the relationship between phonological processes (such as assimilation) and their phonetic basis (such as coarticulation) is rather tenuous (see Anderson 1981). For example, our sMM translation of the original version of the theory due to Clements (1985) implies that the primary indicator of phonemic identity is laryngeal activity – certainly an interesting hypothesis, but perhaps not the most plausible one.

Now that we have a method of expressing hypotheses about feature geometry in a markovian setting, it becomes feasible to translate in the other direction. Given some knowledge about the acoustic domain, we can devise sMMs (and thus indirectly feature geometries) that capture this knowledge. For instance, if we know that the intervals most easily distinguishable in the acoustic signal are silence vs. vowels vs. fricatives vs. stop bursts vs. stop aspiration, we can describe these by a new set of major class features to be placed at the top of the feature geometry. Further, if we know that changes in voicing and nasality will largely be synchronized with these intervals, this suggests cascading i.e. subordination of these features to the major class node, leading to the sMM shown in (10) below:

(10)

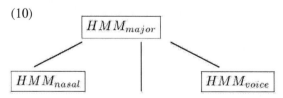

As can be seen from (10), the top level model HMM_{major} receives information about voicing, nasality, and directly from the signal. Since voicing and nasality decisions are relatively easy to make, HMM_{voice} and HMM_{nasal} should be two state models (with no 0th state). But the HMM_{major} model at the top should probably contain a 0th state in addition to the five given by silence, vowels, fricatives, stop bursts, and stop aspiration, since the endpoints of these intervals are not always easy to find. Only a minimum of synchronization should be enforced. Silence and aspiration must be unvoiced (and perhaps oral), and vowels must be voiced[16].

Since the design in (10) is rather speculative, it is perhaps worth emphasizing that the method can be, and indeed should be, applied to acoustic knowledge embodied in the parameters of Markov models. This approach was pioneered in the HMM setting by Poritz 1982 who trained a small (5 state) ergodic model and characterized the resulting output distributions as "strong voicing vs. silence vs. nasal, liquid vs. stop burst, post silence vs. frication". Training an sMM such as (10) in which voicing and nasality are decoupled from the major class features would probably lead to a sharper characterization of the resulting major classes and would pave the way to more realistic acoustic feature models.

5.3.6 Subsequent work

A key issue in the design of sMMs is to decide which models have direct access to the signal and which rely only on the states of other models. Brugnara et al. 1992 developed an asymmetrical arrangement in which one model, the "master", accesses the signal, and a second model, the "slave", has its parameters conditioned both on the signal and the state of the master. The master can be a simple ergodic feature model (they use nasality as an example) and the slave, a vowel model with the standard left-to-right topology.

In our terms, master-slave models are a special case of (freely aligned) direct products. Though Brugnara et al. (1992) note the direct product

---

[16]This does not mean that vowels must be voiced throughout, only that the detection of an unvoiced frame by HMM_{voice} forces HMM_{major} out of the vowel state.

decomposition, their model is conceptualized very differently from the view presented here. First, they perform training over unsegmented data. From our perspective this is a limitation (such training is only possible in the freely aligned case), but it must be said that the case for preferring training methods based on unsegmented data is very strong. Second, they envision the same master conditioning several slaves, while in the sMMs sketched above several masters would simultaneously condition a single slave. While the fundamental idea of reducing the number of parameters to be estimated by structuring the parameter space itself is the same, the relative effectiveness of the two approaches can be quite different, and at this point it would make little sense to speculate about the outcome of such a comparison.

The ongoing project first described in Deng and Erler 1992 has long-term goals very similar to the ones described earlier in this chapter. As the authors put it (p. 3059):

> it is in our long-term interest to verify the validity and useful-
> ness of particular feature representations and to eventually
> arrive at an optimal feature representation (...). In contrast
> to other proposed methods for feature representations where
> features are mapped to phonetic outputs or are extracted
> directly from the speech signal in a deterministic manner
> (Meng and Zue 1991, Howitt 1990), our new method treats
> the feature representation as the underlying process that is
> not directly observable.

The model is implemented in a way that uses neither direct product nor cascade decomposition. Features are taken to be n-ary (with no underspecification), and each combination of different values for different features is made to correspond to a state in a standard HMM. These states are interpreted as *transitional* microsegments as opposed to the *target* microsegments used in the earlier model (Deng, Lennig and Mermelstein 1990). Word models are built from sequences of target microsegments with carefully selected transitional microsegments interdigitated. As the authors note, the new design makes it possible to share training data not only for target but also for transitional microsegments.

In our terms, the only variety of interval structures that fit into this model are interval systems with their attendant MINDUR condition (see (7.3) in section 4.2). Therefore, the warp-averaging problem discussed in section 5.2 above is still present, since different feature lags below the temporal resolution of the system (which is determined by the frame rate) are still averaged together. In the absence of experimental data it would be futile to speculate about the impact of warp-averaging on the performance of the system, but, if training data is available in abundance, the size of the effect can be estimated by increasing the frame rate while keeping the architecture constant[17].

5.4 Conclusions

How do the structured Markov models presented in the previous section avoid the problems with features that we started out with? The fact that features lack reliable acoustic cues is a fact about our conscious knowledge of the matter, not about the objective reality of the situation. Absence of evidence is not evidence of absence. Training for features, though requiring pre-segmented and labeled data, is certainly feasible, and promises to be an efficient way of gathering data about such cues. The issue of zero-one decisions is reflected in the transition probabilities of the models, which were set externally (i.e. not by training) in the manner described in 5.3. Finally, the lack of additivity in different cues for different features is remedied by the cascading mechanism which is at the heart of the system. Since at the leaves of the tree, each feature model receives the same sequence of content vectors, there is no need to selectively pre-emphasize some aspect of the signal to bring out one feature at the expense of the others.

---

[17]But with contravariant changes in the number of states, see 3.4.1 above.

The power of the system comes not only from its trainability, but also from the delayed decision-making mechanism built into it. Let us suppose, for the sake of the argument, that the machines at the leaves cannot be trained for better performance than the expertise-based feature detectors, so that the decision on any individual feature is only 60-70% reliable. The machines at class nodes can still be more reliable, since their decisions are based on the combined effects of the subordinate machines, so that restrictions on the *dynamic* cooccurrence of features can be exploited. This way, the higher a class node, the more reliable the decision made by it, so that at the top (root) level decisions might turn out to be more reliable than the decisions made by segment models. Finally, above the segment level, decisions can benefit from the knowledge of lexicon and syntax, if such knowledge is available, just as in standard systems.

Needless to say, the considerable theoretical support sMMs receive from autosegmental phonology is no guarantee of success. sMMs can still fail, both as instruments of comparing linguistic theories and as speech recognition devices. They will probably fail to provide consistent results across languages, meaning that they will have to be used with a great deal of caution in evaluating theories based on typological evidence, but if they fail to provide consistent results even for a single language, they cannot be used for the intended purpose of comparing and evaluating phonological hypotheses at all. Failure in speech recognition is an even simpler matter. If sMMs are outperformed by ordinary HMMs, they have failed. But here a word of caution is in order: performance evaluation should be based on open vocabulary, not on closed vocabulary tasks.

Human "speech recognizers" operate very efficiently at the margin where no lexical or syntactic knowledge is available. They are capable of recognizing words such as proper names that they have seen but never heard before, and of acquiring, and even transcribing, words they have never heard *or* seen before. Inasmuch as this capability is an important, in fact necessary, component of language acquisition, no system that lacks this capability can be an adequate model of human linguistic competence. Even more strongly, among two systems, *ceteris paribus,* the one that displays this capability to a larger extent is the better model of human linguistic ability. Thus I would like to conclude that the criteria of adequacy employed by the linguist and the speech engineer are not at all incompatible.

Speech engineers, having made 95% of the progress that can be made on closed vocabulary systems, will of sheer necessity be more and more sympathetic to the view that the performance of their systems is determined at the margin, not at the center, of the vocabulary. Linguists, who insist that their enterprise is a scientific one, will have to become comfortable with the idea that of two models, other factors being equal, the one that *does* better, *is* better. It seems to me that there is no reason to be afraid of a straight comparison. While it is true that the linearly structured, statistical models of the speech engineers presently do better than the sequentially structured, expertise-based models built by linguists or linguistically minded speech engineers, the gap is not as wide as it might appear from evaluations based on closed vocabulary, and with the introduction of the kind of hybrid feature-based systems proposed here, it might be closed within a few years.

5.5 References

Anderson, Stephen R. 1981. Why phonology isn't "natural". *Linguistic Inquiry* **12** 493–540.

Bahl, L.R., P.V. de Souza, P.S. Gopalakrishnan, D. Nahamoo and M.A. Picheny 1991. Decision trees for phonological rules in continuous speech. In *ICASSP-91*. Toronto, 185–188.

Baum, L.E., T. Petrie, G. Soules and N. Weiss 1970. A maximization technique occurring in the statistical analysis of probabilistic functions of Markov chains. *Annals of Mathematical Statistics* **41** 164–171.

Bridle, John S. 1990. Alpha-Nets: a recurrent 'neural' network architecture with a Hidden Markov Model interpretation. *Speech Communication* **9** 83–92.

Brown, Peter, John Cocke, Stephen Della Pietra, Vincent J. Della Pietra, Fredrick Jelinek, John D. Lafferty, Robert L. Mercer and Paul S. Roossin 1990. A statistical approach to machine translation. *Computational Linguistics* **16** 79–85.

Brugnara, F., R. De Mori, D. Giulinai and M. Omologo 1992. A family of parallel Hidden Markov Models. *ICASSP-92* **I** 377–380.

Chomsky, Noam 1957. *Syntactic Structures*. Mouton, The Hague.

Church, Kenneth W. 1983. *Phrase-structure parsing: a method for taking advantage of allophonic constraints*. PhD Thesis, MIT.

Church, Kenneth W. 1988. A stochastic parts program and noun phrase parser for unrestricted text. In *Proceedings of the Second Conference on Applied NLP*.

Clements, George N. 1985. The geometry of phonological features. *Phonology Yearbook* **2** 225–252.

Cole, Ronald A., Michael S. Phillips, Robert Brennan, Ben Chigier, Rich Green, Robert Weide and Janet Weaver 1986. Status of the C-MU phonetic classification system. In *Proc DARPA Speech Recognition Workshop*. Palo Alto, CA, 1–5.

Cole, Ronald A., Richard M. Stern, Michael S. Phillips, Scott M. Brill, Andrew P. Pilant and Philippe Specker 1983. Feature-based speaker-independent recognition of isolated English letters. In *ICASSP-83*. Boston, MA, 731–733.

Dempster, A.P., N.M. Laird and D.B. Rubin 1977. Maximum likelihood estimation from incomplete data. *Journal of the Royal Statistical Society (B)* **39** 1–38.

Deng, L. and K. Erler 1992. Structural design of hidden Markov model speech recognizer using multivalued phonetic features: Comparison with segmental speech units. *JASA* **92** 3058–3067.

Deng, L., M. Lennig and P. Mermelstein 1990. Modeling microsegments of stop consonants in a hidden Markov model based word recognizer. *JASA* **87** 2738–2747.

Fujimura, Osamu 1981. Temporal organization of articulatory movements as a multidimensional phrasal structure. *Phonetica* **38** 271–288.

Glass, James R. and Victor W. Zue 1988. Multi-level acoustic segmentation of continuous speech. In *ICASSP-88*. New York, 429–432.

Goldsmith, John A. 1976. *Autosegmental Phonology*. PhD Thesis, MIT.

Good, I.J. 1953. The population frequencies of species and the estimation of population parameters. *Biometrika* **40** 237–264.

Hayes, Bruce 1990. Precompiled phrasal phonology. In *The Phonology-Syntax Connection*, Sharon Inkelas and Draga Zec, (eds.) University of Chicago Press, 77–100.

Howitt, A. 1990. Toward an automatic system for distinctive feature extraction. *JASA Suppl* **88** S102.

Itô, Junko, Armin Mester, Elisabeth Selkirk and Harry van der Hulst 1991. Properties of feature organization, Reading materials for NSF-sponsored Workshop BNS-9021357, LSA Linguistic Institute, UC Santa Cruz.

Jakobson, Roman, Gunnar Fant and Morris Halle 1952. *Preliminaries to speech analysis: the distinctive features and their correlates*. MIT Press, Cambridge MA.

Jelinek, Frederick, Robert Mercer and Salim Roukos 1990. Classifying words for improved statistical language models. In *ICASSP-90*. Albuquerque, NM, 621–624.

Ladefoged, Peter 1971. *Preliminaries to linguistic phonetics.* University of Chicago Press.

Lee, Kai-Fu, Satoru Hayamizu, Hsiao-Wuen Hon, Cecil Huang, Jonathan Swartz and Robert Weide 1990. Allophone clustering for continuous speech recognition. In *ICASSP-90.* Albuquerque, NM, 749–752.

Lee, Kai-Fu, Hsiao-Wuen Hon, Mei-Yuh Hwang and Sanjoy Mahajan 1990. Recent progress and future outlook of the SPHINX speech recognition system. *Computer Speech and Language* **4** 57–69.

Levinson, Stephen E., Mark Y. Liberman, Andrej Ljolje and L.G. Miller 1989. Speaker independent phonetic transcription of fluent speech for large vocabulary speech recognition. In *ICASSP-89.* Glasgow, 441–444.

Makhoul, John and Richard Schwartz 1986. Ignorance modeling. In *Invariance and Variability of Speech Processes*, Joseph S. Perkell and Dennis H. Klatt, (eds.) Lawrence Erlebaum Associates, Hillsdale, NJ, 344–345.

Meng, Helen M. and Victor W. Zue 1991. Signal representation comparision for phonetic classification. In *ICASSP-91.* Toronto, 285–288.

Miller, George A. and Noam Chomsky 1963. Finitary models of language users. In *Handbook of mathematical psychology*, R. Duncan Luce, Robert R. Bush and Eugene Galanter, (eds.) Wiley, New York, 419–491.

Ostendorf, Mari and Salim Ruocos 1989. A stochastic segment model for phoneme-based continuos speech recognition. *IEEE ASSP* **37** 1857–1869.

Pierrehumbert, Janet B. 1980. *The Phonology and Phonetics of English Intonation.* PhD Thesis, MIT.

Pierrehumbert, Janet B. 1981. Synthesizing Intonation. *JASA* **70** 985–95.

Poritz, Alan B. 1982. Linear predictive Hidden Markov models and the speech signal, ICASSP-82, Paris.

Russell, Martin J. and M. K. Moore 1985. Explicit modelling of state occupancy in Hidden Markov Models for automatic speech recognition, ICASSP-85, Tampa, FL.

Varga, A.P. and R.K. Moore 1990. Hidden Markov Model decomposition of speech and noise. In *ICASSP-90*. Albuquerque, NM, 845–848.

Woods, William A., Madelaine Bates, G. Brown, B. Bruce, C. Cook, J. Klovstad, John Makhoul, Bonnie Nash-Webber, Richard Schwartz, J. Wolf and Victor Zue 1976. Speech understanding systems: final technical progress report, Bolt Beranek and Newman Inc. Report 3438, Cambridge MA.

Young, S.J. 1990. Competitive training in Hidden Markov Models. In *ICASSP-90*. Albuquerque, NM, 681–684.

Index of definitions

Index of authors